U0071374

飛越
太平洋的
友情 與美國國會議員的書信集

仉家彪　著

Introduction

With all humbleness, I am greatly honored to write this introduction to C. P. Chang's collection of correspondence with American friends in the U. S. Congress, many of which dated back well over thirty years ago. As a former Research Fellow at the Institute of International Relations, National Chengchi University, focusing my research on American foreign policy toward East Asia and Pacific region in general and on American relations with the Republic of China in particular, the name C. P. Chang has not been totally a stranger to me though we never got acquainted then. We subsequently became intimate friend as regular churchgoers in Grace Baptist Church, Taipei.

My accumulated knowledge about his various and fascinating careers in the government and the private sector derived from the weekly chat with him and several other like-minded friends such as Eddie Yu and Huang Guo-erh, at Starbucks Coffee Shop at the corner of Round Circle on Ming Sheng East Road. The weekly rendezvous there becomes a mini club for exchanging views and ideas and for leisure talks, so to speak. We were always captivated by his interesting recounting of the years of service and experience as First Secretary at the ROC Embassy at Washington, D. C., especially in liaising with U. S. senators, congressmen and their staff assistants, many of them subsequently became bosom friends of C. P. even after his retirement from public service. C. P. also won recognition for his dedication and contribution in his outstanding career in private sector, proving himself a man of all seasons.

This collection of correspondence is more than just an exchange of letters among friends across the Pacific. They are living testimonies to some of the important events in US-ROC relations of the period. And C. P. has given a clear picture of it as an insider. He has set a fine example for young and zealous ROC diplomats stationed abroad and eager to win friends for their country.

Indeed, even long after retiring from government service, his diplomatic talent and finesse were again called upon when the ROC Government suddenly had to cope with the crisis arising from the Carter administration's abrupt and unilateral termination of diplomatic relations with Taipei to recognize the Beijing regime, as well as the pending drafting of the Taiwan Relations Act by the U. S. Congress to maintain US-ROC bilateral and substantial relations intact in the post-derecognized period. This was an extraordinary challenging task for C. P. to show his mettle in safeguarding Taiwan's legitimate national interests and national security amid the changing power politics in the region.

C. P. has every right to look back on those years of uphill tasks and accomplishments with some measure of gratification, satisfaction and pride. Indeed, he has served his country and his people well. This collection of correspondence also bespeaks his fine personal traits as a caring and loving husband, an attentive and kind father, a loyal and dependable friend, a dedicated public serviceman, and a devoted believer of his faith. To borrow what the Apostle Paul had summarized and testified about his lifelong missionary struggle, it can be said in a similar vein that C. P. Chang has truly "fought the good fight"—even to the last ditch.

David C. L. Auw

April 12, 2011

Taipei

Contents

Introduction / *David C. L. Auw* 3

1970s

January 21, 1974 / *Sherwood L. Boehlert* 12

January 30, 1974 / *Ellis C. Stewart* 13

February 12, 1974 / *Sherwood L. Boehlert* 14

May 3, 1974 / *Charles D. Bigler* 15

May 10, 1974 / *Ron Meredith* 16

May 16, 1974 / *Hite McLaen* 17

July 10, 1974 / *David A. Rust* 18

July 12, 1974 / *David A. Rust* 19

July 26, 1974 / *C. P. Chang* 20

March 13, 1975 / *Eiler Ravnholt* 23

March 14, 1975 / *David A. Keene* 24

April 17, 1975 / *Roger A. Keats* 25

June 10, 1975 / *Richard S. Williamson* 26

July 7, 1975 / *Richard S. Williamson* 27

August 27, 1975 / *Sally A. Shelton* 28

September 4, 1975 / *Charles W. Bergstorm* 29

September 17, 1975 / *Sandra D. Hanbury* 30

September 19, 1975 / *Charles W. McBride* 31

October 2, 1975 / *Dawson Mathis* 32

October 20, 1975 / *Richard S. Williamson* 33

October 22, 1975 / *George W. Pritts* 34

December 1, 1975 / *Geoffrey G. Peterson* 35

December 17, 1975 / *Richard S. Williamson* 36

January 5, 1976 / *George W. Pritts* 37

January 7, 1976 / *Richard S. Williamson* 38

January 26, 1976 / *H. A. Gilliam, Jr.* 39

February 6, 1976 / *Harrison Loesch* 40

February 16, 1976 / *Herb Wadsworth* 41

February 24, 1976 / *Ron Schrader* 42

February 27, 1976 / *Donald L. Robinson* 43

May 3, 1976 / *James C. Webster* 44

May 13, 1976 / *Janet B. Watlington* 45

May 26, 1976 / *D. Eileen Nixon* 46

June 4, 1976 / *Richard S. Williamson* 47

June 5, 1976 / *Richard S. Williamson* 48

July 20, 1976 / *Richard S. Williamson* 49

September 14, 1976 / *Pamela Dale Synder* 50

October 7, 1976 / *Coleman J. Conroy* 51

October 29, 1976 / *Walt Evans* 52

January 5, 1977 / Janet B. Watlington 53

January 18, 1977 / C. P. Chang 54

January 27, 1977 / Richard Moe 55

February 3, 1977 / C. P. Chang 56

February 24, 1977 / Richard Moe 58

February 3, 1977 / J. Terry Emerson 59

December 9, 1977 / Richard (Dick) Stone 61

January 24, 1978 / Richard (Dick) Stone 62

March 1, 1978 / Walter D. Huddleston 63

March 2, 1978 / John Sparkman 64

March 2, 1978 / John Glenn 65

March 2, 1978 / Herman E. Talmadge 66

March 2, 1978 / Sally A. Shelton 67

March 3, 1978 / Sherwood L. Boehlert 68

March 3, 1978 / J. Terry Emerson 69

March 3, 1978 / Eileen Nixon 70

March 3, 1978 / Barry Goldwater 71

March 6, 1978 / Richard Moe 72

March 6, 1978 / Michael R. McLeod 73

March 8, 1978 / James O. Eastland 74

March 8, 1978 / Howard H. Baker, Jr. 75

March 8, 1978 / Jim Wright 76

March 8, 1978 / Roy A. Werner 77

March 9, 1978 / Michael Stern 78

March 13, 1978 / Jack McDonald 79

March 14, 1978 / Richard (Dick) Stone 80

March 14, 1978 / George A. Dalley 81

March 15, 1978 / Lisbeth K. Godley 83

March 20, 1978 / Gene E. Godley 84

March 20, 1978 / Edward T. Martin 85

March 21, 1978 / G. Cranwell Montgomery 86

March 22, 1978 / Don Fuqua 87

April 3, 1978 / C. Dayle Henington 88

April 20, 1978 / Richard (Dick) Stone 89

May 24, 1978 / Roy A. Werner 90

July 14, 1978 / Richard (Dick) Stone 91

July 26, 1978 / Barry Goldwater 92

August 7, 1978 / Y. S. Sun 93

August 22 ,1978 / Barry Goldwater 95

October 28, 1978 / John Glenn 96

June 19, 1979 / C. P. Chang 97

July 9, 1979 / Richard Moe 100

July 17, 1979 / C. P. Chang 101

July 30, 1979 / Richard Moe 102

October 4, 1979 / Richard Moe 104

September 11, 1979 / Richard (Dick) Stone 105

1980s

May 20, 1983 / *Richard S. Williamson* 108

December 25, 1986 / *Dick and Ann Dingman* 109

1990s

October 29, 1991 / *J. Terry Emerson* 112

December 31, 1992 / *J. Terry Emerson* 113

January 20, 1993 / *C. P. Chang* 114

February 5, 1993 / *J. Terry Emerson* 116

December 8, 1992 / *Charles R. O'Regan* 117

January 13, 1993 / *C. P. Chang* 118

January 18, 1993 / *C. P. Chang* 119

January 20, 1993 / *C. P. Chang* 121

February 28, 1994 / *C. Dayle Henington* 123

March 18, 1994 / *C. P. Chang* 124

September 20-22, 1993 / *C. P. Chang* 126

June 16, 1994 / *C. Dayle Henington* 132

October 27, 1994 / *Marshall L. Lynam* 133

August 8, 1994 / *C. Dayle Henington* 134

June 30, 1994 / *C. Dayle Henington* 135

January 7, 1995 / *C. Dayle Henington* 136

May 23, 1995 / *C. Dayle Henington* 138

June 21, 1995 / *C. Dayle Henington* 139

December 20, 1995 / *C. Dayle Henington* 140

January 12, 1996 / *C. P. Chang* 141

August 12, 1996 / *C. Dayle Henington* 142

May 25, 1996 / *William H. Edington* 143

July 3, 1996 / *C. P. Chang* 144

October 30, 1996 / *C. Dayle Henington* 146

December 17, 1996 / *C. Dayle Henington* 147

September 28, 1997 / *C. Dayle Henington* 148

June 12, 1999 / *Marshall L. Lynam* 149

June 21, 1999 / *C. P. Chang* 150

2000s

February 1, 2000 / *C. P. Chang* 154

May 27, 2003 / *C. Dayle Henington* 156

June 12, 2003 / *C. P. Chang* 158

July 15, 2003 / *C. Dayle Henington* 159

August 2, 2006 / *C. Dayle Henington* 160

October 12, 2006 / *C. P. Chang* 161

November 1, 2006 / *C. Dayle Henington* 165

January 29, 2008 / *C. Dayle Henington* 166

December 8, 2009 / *C. Dayle Henington* 167

February 21, 2010 / *C. P. Chang* 168

1970s

一九七一年十月二十五日，聯合國大會通過第二七五八號決議，正式決定由中華人民共和國取代中華民國，成為在聯合國代表中國的政府。該決議宣稱「中華人民共和國政府是聯合國內代表中國的唯一合法代表」，而各國則相繼與中華民國政府斷交，轉與中華人民共和國建交。

伴隨著中華民國的聯合國席位被中華人民共和國取代、美國等國斷交等接續而來的外交挫跌，使台灣喪失了國際上的外交主權。美國撤離軍援與經援，外加能源危機與國際糧荒使台灣賴以支撐的經濟成長面臨大幅的衰退，與一九五〇年代的台海戰爭相比，一九七〇年代的台灣面臨另一種型態的維繫存亡考驗。

一九七〇年，作者仇家彪（C. P. Chang）先生擔任中華民國經濟部孫運璿部長英文秘書。

一九七一至一九七三年，仇家彪先生擔任中華民國交通部觀光局主任秘書。

一九七三年，仇家彪先生擔任中華民國外交部北美司專門委員。

一九七四至一九七八年，仇家彪先生擔任中華民國駐美大使館一等秘書、參事。

一九七八年，仇家彪先生擔任中華造船公司副總經理。

一九七九年，仇家彪先生擔任華美企業集團海外開發公司總經理。

DONALD J. MITCHELL
31st DISTRICT, NEW YORK

COMMITTEE:
ARMED SERVICES

1527 LONGWORTH HOUSE
OFFICE BUILDING
WASHINGTON, D.C. 20515
TELEPHONE (202) 225-3665

Congress of the United States
House of Representatives
Washington, D.C. 20515

January 21, 1974

Mr. Chang Chia-piao, Senior Specialist
North American Affairs Department
Ministry of Foreign Affairs
2, Chieh Shou Road, Taipei
Republic of China

Dear "CP":

Now that I've had an opportunity to pause for a moment to reflect upon the events of the past two weeks I want to pass along
two pertinent observations.

First, I am tremendously impressed by the Republic of China
success story which is continuing despite recent international
diplomatic reverses. Second, I am convinced that the dedication,
determination, devotion to duty and good old-fashioned hard work
of truly fine people like Chang Chia-piao are responsible for that
ROC success story and will be instrumental in adding still more
favorable chapters.

You helped make my visit to the Republic one of the most memorable experiences of my life and I sincerely thank you. I'm pleased
that our paths crossed, but I'm even more pleased that there will
shortly be an opportunity for our families to meet. I look forward
to a lasting friendship, CP, and I hope you will let me know as soon
as your travel arrangements are complete so we will be able to com-
mence planning for our get-together here in Washington.

Sincerely,

Sherwood L. Boehlert
Executive Assistant

SLB:v

P.S. — Please do let me know when you're
coming to Washington — I would like the
Chang family to join us for some American
hospitality. My daughter, like yours, is a young teenager (13)

12

JOHN SPARKMAN, ALA., CHAIRMAN

WILLIAM PROXMIRE, WIS.   JOHN TOWER, TEX.
HARRISON A. WILLIAMS, JR., N.J.   WALLACE F. BENNETT, UTAH
THOMAS J. MC INTYRE, N.H.   EDWARD W. BROOKE, MASS.
ALAN CRANSTON, CALIF.   BOB PACKWOOD, OREG.
ADLAI E. STEVENSON III, ILL.   BILL BROCK, TENN.
J. BENNETT JOHNSTON, JR., LA.   ROBERT TAFT, JR., OHIO
WILLIAM D. HATHAWAY, MAINE   LOWELL P. WEICKER, JR., CONN.
JOSEPH R. BIDEN, JR., DEL.

DUDLEY L. O'NEAL, JR.
STAFF DIRECTOR AND GENERAL COUNSEL

United States Senate

COMMITTEE ON BANKING, HOUSING AND URBAN AFFAIRS
WASHINGTON, D.C. 20510

January 30, 1974

Mr. C. P. Chang
North American Affairs Department
Ministry of Foreign Affairs
Taipei, Taiwan
Republic of China

Dear C. P.:

I have written to the persons on the lists which you furnished
me to express my great appreciation for all the assistance which was
given to us while we were in the Republic of China and ~~before~~ the
briefings which we enjoyed while there.

I just want to add a personal word of thanks to you. I have
told everyone that your conduct was outstanding.

Incidentally, Minister Hu tells me that you may be in Washington
soon. I hope that this is correct as it will give me an opportunity
to return some of your hospitality.

Sincerely, and with every good wish,

Ellis C. Stewart
Executive Secretary to
Senator John Sparkman

Let me know.

13

HOUSE OF REPRESENTATIVES

WASHINGTON, D. C. 20515

MORGAN F. MURPHY
SECOND DISTRICT
ILLINOIS

February 12, 1974

Mr. C. P. Chang
North American Affairs Department
Ministry of Foreign Affairs
Taipei, Taiwan
Republic of China

Dear "C.P.":

Sorry for the delay in dropping
you a note of my sincere thanks for your courtesy
and assistance during the group's trip to Taiwan.

I trust you and your family are
in good health and I understand from Mr. Hu that
you will soon be in Washington. It will be good
seeing you.

Work here in the office has been
really hectic and I am just now getting things
back into routine.

Hong Kong, Tokyo and Hawaii were
great, especially Hawaii. I will tell you all about
it when I see you.

Haven't finished your book yet,
but am enjoying it. How are you coming on the one
I gave you?

With warm regards,

Ann

14

JOHN E. HUNT
1ST DISTRICT, NEW JERSEY

COMMITTEE:
ARMED SERVICES

NANCY SOHL
ADMINISTRATIVE ASSISTANT

Congress of the United States
House of Representatives
Washington, D.C. 20515

WASHINGTON OFFICE:
ROOM 1440
LONGWORTH BUILDING
TELEPHONE: 225-6501

CAMDEN DISTRICT OFFICE:
114 N. 7TH STREET
CAMDEN, NEW JERSEY
TELEPHONE: 365-4442

GLOUCESTER COUNTY OFFICE:
67 COOPER STREET
WOODBURY, NEW JERSEY
TELEPHONE: 845-0200

May 3, 1974

Mr. C.P. Chiang
Embassy of the Republic of China
Washington, D.C. 20008

Dear C.P.:

I didn't want to call you this week as I can imagine just how busy you have been home-hunting. My agents of course have told me that you arrived in the office on Monday, and that your family was arriving Thursday. I'll bet you'll be glad to have them with you.

C.P. I do want to thank you ever so much for a most rewarding trip. Everywhere we went everyone was so kind and most gracious. The people of your country have a great deal of pride and that impressed me very much. I must say C.P. that I came home sharing that same feeling.

As for yourself, beside being a good friend, you are a "tour guide extraordinaire". I hope we didn't give you too many headaches. If so, I'm sorry!

Sometime in the near future, perhaps when our swimming pool opens later this month, we'd like to have you and your family to the house for an afternoon of eating, swimming, and perhaps something cold to drink. I'll give you a call about that soon.

In the meantime thanks again for the most wonderful trip. Hope to see you soon,

With personal regards,

Chuck

Charles D. Bigler
Asst. to John E. Hunt, M.C.

15

JAMES O. EASTLAND, MISS., CHAIRMAN

JOHN L. MC CLELLAN, ARK.   ROMAN L. HRUSKA, NEBR.
SAM J. ERVIN, JR., N.C.   HIRAM L. FONG, HAWAII
PHILIP A. HART, MICH.   HUGH SCOTT, PA.
EDWARD M. KENNEDY, MASS.   STROM THURMOND, S.C.
BIRCH BAYH, IND.   MARLOW W. COOK, KY.
QUENTIN N. BURDICK, N. DAK.   CHARLES MC C. MATHIAS, JR., MD.
ROBERT C. BYRD, W. VA.   EDWARD J. GURNEY, FLA.
JOHN V. TUNNEY, CALIF.

JOHN H. HOLLOMAN III
CHIEF COUNSEL AND STAFF DIRECTOR

United States Senate

COMMITTEE ON THE JUDICIARY
WASHINGTON, D.C. 20510

May 10, 1974

Mr. C. P. Chang
Chinese Embassy
2340 Massachusetts Avenue N.W.
Washington, D.C.

Dear C. P.:

Although words can never sufficiently repay you for the many kindnesses you extended me, I wanted to thank you for all your assistance during my visit to the Republic of China.

Your contribution to the success of our trip was immense. As the representative of your government most directly responsible for our group, you did a superb job.

I wish you, Cecilia, and your daughter every success as you begin your tour of duty in the United States. If I can be of assistance to you in any way, please do not hesitate to call upon me.

Thanks again for everything.

Sincerely,

Ron Meredith
Legislative Assistant to
Senator Marlow W. Cook

P. S. I hope Cecilia and I can make a Baptist out of you during your stay in the U.S.A.!

16

JAMES O. EASTLAND, MISS., CHAIRMAN

JOHN L. MC CLELLAN, ARK.   ROMAN L. HRUSKA, NEBR.
SAM J. ERVIN, JR., N.C.   HIRAM L. FONG, HAWAII
PHILIP A. HART, MICH.   HUGH SCOTT, PA.
EDWARD M. KENNEDY, MASS.   STROM THURMOND, S.C.
BIRCH BAYH, IND.   MARLOW W. COOK, KY.
QUENTIN N. BURDICK, N. DAK.   CHARLES MC C. MATHIAS, JR., MD.
ROBERT C. BYRD, W. VA.   EDWARD J. GURNEY, FLA.
JOHN V. TUNNEY, CALIF.

JOHN H. HOLLOMAN III
CHIEF COUNSEL AND STAFF DIRECTOR

United States Senate

COMMITTEE ON THE JUDICIARY
WASHINGTON, D.C. 20510

May 16, 1974

Second Secretary C. P. Chang
Embassy of China
2311 Massachusetts Avenue, N.W.
Washington, D.C. 20008

Dear C. P.:

I enjoyed seeing you again today at lunch and just wanted to thank you again for everything you did for all of us while we were in the Republic of China. You know that my words will never be able to express my appreciation for your and your country's gracious hospitality. I look forward to seeing you again soon.

Sincerely,

Hite McLean
Professional Staff Member

17

WARREN G. MAGNUSON, WASH., CHAIRMAN

JOHN O. PASTORE, R.I.   NORRIS COTTON, N.H.
VANCE HARTKE, IND.   JAMES B. PEARSON, KANS.
PHILIP A. HART, MICH.   ROBERT P. GRIFFIN, MICH.
HOWARD W. CANNON, NEV.   HOWARD H. BAKER, JR., TENN.
RUSSELL B. LONG, LA.   MARLOW W. COOK, KY.
FRANK E. MOSS, UTAH   TED STEVENS, ALASKA
ERNEST F. HOLLINGS, S.C.   J. GLENN BEALL, JR., MD.
DANIEL K. INOUYE, HAWAII
JOHN V. TUNNEY, CALIF.
ADLAI E. STEVENSON III, ILL.

FREDERICK J. LORDAN, STAFF DIRECTOR
MICHAEL PERTSCHUK, CHIEF COUNSEL

United States Senate

COMMITTEE ON COMMERCE

WASHINGTON, D.C. 20510

July 10, 1974

His Excellency James C. H. Shen, Ambassador
Extraordinary & Plenipotentiary
Embassy of the Republic of China
2311 Massachusetts Avenue
Washington, D. C. 20008

Dear Mr. Ambassador:

I would like to take this opportunity to thank you for all of the kindness and hospitality that you and your government have extended to me in recent months.

Needless to say, it was a great pleasure for me to meet you during the recent luncheon you hosted for Congressional staff members who visited the Republic of China in April. I would also be remiss if I did not sincerely thank you, Minister S. K. Hu, and Secretary C. P. Chen gave us in making our visit to Taiwan possible. The briefing sessions and the tours of various projects around Taiwan have significantly contributed to my understanding of the social-economic-political and military institutions of the Republic of China. This visit certainly contributed to my understanding of the current situation on Taiwan, and I have briefed Senator Beall in considerable detail relative to this matter.

Thank you once again for your assistance in making this visit possible.

Sincerely,

David A. Rust
Legislative Assistant

DAR/ls

18

J. GLENN BEALL, JR.
MARYLAND

COMMITTEES:
COMMERCE
LABOR AND PUBLIC WELFARE
SENATE SELECT COMMITTEE
ON SMALL BUSINESS
SPECIAL COMMITTEE ON AGING

United States Senate
WASHINGTON, D.C. 20510

July 12, 1974

C. P. Chen, First Secretary
Embassy of the Republic of China
2311 Massachusetts Avenue
Washington, D. C.   20008

Dear C. P.:

I would like to take this opportunity to extend
my belated thanks to you for the contribution you made
to the success of our April visit to the Republic of
China and for all the hospitality you have shown me
since your arrival in this country.

The total success of our visit to Taiwan was
largely due to your meticulous planning prior to our
arrival and your tireless efforts on our behalf throughout our visit to the Republic of China. The briefing
sessions and the tours of various projects around Taiwan
have significantly contributed to my understanding of the
social-economic-political and military institutions of
the Republic of China. This visit certainly contributed
to my understanding of the current situation on Taiwan,
and I have briefed Senator Beall in considerable detail
relative to this matter.

As one who had never been to Asia before, I can
honestly say that I benefited greatly from the firsthand
observation I was able to make throughout your nation.
I have also come to value very highly our personal friendship, and I look forward to introducing you to a number
of my friends and colleagues in the not too distant future.

Let me close by once again thanking you for the
outstanding effort you made in insuring the success of
the April visit of our Congressional staff delegation.

Sincerely,

David A. Rust
Legislative Assistant

DAR/mhb

19

Embassy of the Republic of China
Washington, D. C. 20008

July 26, 1974

Mr. Charles D. Bigler
Room 1440
Longworth Building
House of Representatives
Washington, D.C. 20510

Dear Chuck:

I want to thank you very sincerely for your thoughtfulness in sending me clippings from the Congressional Record
from time to time. As a reminder, they have been extremely
useful to me.

On reading your letter of July 24, 1974 to Minister Hu
on your views of Senator Jackson's recent statement, I recall
Lord Palmerston's prescription for Great Britain in the 19th
century. He said: "We have no eternal allies, and we have no
eternal enemies. Our interests are eternal and perpetual,
and those interests it is our duty to follow." Did Senator
Jackson's various statements sound like an echo of this English
gentleman?

Well, in the abstract this guide to national policy and
behavior is sound enough. But there is a problem. In dealing with one's national interests, one cannot avoid involve-
ment in the interests of others--involvement in ways and with
intensities that sometimes work massive influence on the lives
and welfares of those who are the objects of one's policy.

To sum up the U.S.-ROC relations in the past twenty-five
years, I would like to give you some facts about what had
happened during this period:

1. By the end of 1949, the Republic of China was written
off by the U.S. Government as the Communist troops had overrun
the mainland. The general attitude of the time is clear in
the report "United States Relations with China--the so-called
White Paper."

2. Less than six months later, President Truman announced
in the statement of June 27, 1950: "The attack upon Korea makes
it plain beyond all doubts that Communism has beyond the use of
subversion to conquer independent nations..... In these circum-

stances, the occupation of Formosa by Communist forces would
be a direct threat to the security of the Pacific area and
to the United States forces performing their lawful and ne-
cessary functions in that area. Accordingly, I have ordered
the Seventh Fleet to prevent any attack on Formosa." The
shift in position is clear enough. As an act in the interest
of American security in the situation must be seen as reason-
able and prudent.

.3. On the occassion of the signing of the Mutual Defense
Treaty in 1954, Secretary of State Dulles stated: "It is my
hope that the signing of this Defense Treaty will put to rest
once and for all rumors and reports that the United States
will in any manner agree to the abandonment of Formosa and
Pescadores to Communist control."

4. In a speech given in Japan on January 28, 1964, Dean
Rusk, Secretary of State, in describing American policy said:
"We will never abandon the 12 million people on Taiwan to
Communist tyrany. We support the National Government of Taiwan, recognize it as the legitimate spokesman of the Chinese
people, and will continue to support it in the U.N. and else-
where." We can see a shift in the content of public statements,
veering from the single declaration of Taiwan's security role
in U.S. strategy and reaching toward a broader commitment--
support for the political entity of the ROC.

5. During the Vietnam War, the United States was getting
some use from facilities on Taiwan in logistic support. This
represented the first real use of Taiwan for extensive military purposes since the Korean War.

6. Nixon, after Shanghai Communique, in a broadcast from
Los Angeles on July 15, 1971 said: "Our action in seeking a
new relationship with the PRC will not be at the expense of
old friends." On Feb. 9, 1972 he said to the Congress in his
report "U.S. Foreign Policy for the 1970's": "With the Republic
of China, we shall maintain our friendship, our diplomatic ties
and our defense commitment."

7. To sum up again; the U.S. had, in a statement made by
President Truman on Jan. 5, 1950, put forward a position that
expressed a "hand off" policy toward ROC taking refugee on
Taiwan. This was followed by massive and consistent support--
military, economic and political. Twenty-five years and over

5 billion U.S. dollars later, there stands Taiwan. The 15 million people who lived there were made dependents of the United States. What was done was done in what was seen at the time as service to the security to the United States.

It is pointless to argue the rights and wrongs of the U.S. China policy, or to think that the U.S. Government can now cause to vanish all that has been said and done. We are where we are. In the process of getting there, the U.S. had defined our place in the world. Nations grow and change and time can work its way. Nevertheless, American moral duty is clear. It would be the tragedy of this century, if the euphoria of accomodation with the Chinese Communists on mainland led actions that impose an unwelcome solution on the people on Taiwan in the interest of new concepts of United States Strategy.

The above thinking has come across my mind many times in the past, when reflecting on turbulent events of the last twenty-five years in our struggle to maintain freedom on Taiwan. The heartwarming sentiments expressed in your letter toward my country and my people, however, inspired me to write down my feelings. As I always have great confidence in American decency in the political games, I am completely in agreement with your remarks in the letter:"A vast majority of Americans would favor your position over that of the Communists on mainland. They just have never been asked."

I am now asking you to give me your frank comments on my summing-up of U.S.-ROC relations. Do you think I should pass it to my friends on the congressional staff for reference? I would very much appreciate hearing your comments.

With all best wishes,

Sincerely,

C. P. Chang

C. P. Chang

DANIEL K. INOUYE
HAWAII

United States Senate
WASHINGTON, D.C. 20510

March 13, 1975

Mr. C. P. Chang
Embassy of China
2311 Massachusetts Avenue
Washington, D. C. 20008

Dear C. P.:

Attached is the article from the March 4th STAR-BULLETIN which
I promised to bring to your attention. I personally question whether
the 1976 campaign will fought on the issue of the future of our relationship with the Republic of China but I suppose it could evolve into a
minor issue, at least under certain circumstances.

Aloha,

EILER RAVNHOLT
Administrative Assistant

ER:bhm
Enclosure

23

United States Senate

WASHINGTON, D.C. 20510

March 14, 1975

Mr. C. P. Chang
First Secretary
Embassy of the Republic
   of China
2311 Massachusetts Avenue, N.W.
Washington, D. C. 20008

Dear C. P.:

I just wanted to let you know that both Karlyn and I really enjoyed the recent gathering at your home. The food and the company were excellent and I do hope that we will be all able to get together again from time to time.

Thank you again for having us.

With best personal regards,

Sincerely,

David A. Keene
Executive Assistant to
Senator James L. Buckley

April 17, 1975

Mr C. P. Chang
First Secretary
Embassy, Republic of China
2311 Massachusetts Ave   NW
Washington, D. C.   20008

Dear C. P.

Here is the $84 that I owe you. I greatly appreciated that $100, since
I was so thoroughly enjoying buying half of your country's GNP. It was
worth every penny I spent, but why so many pennies?

I look forward to lunch next tuesday, 1230 at the Monocle. At that
time I will suggest several names that you might want to have visit your
country. Some will be conservatives and several will be from liberal
offices. I feel, as you do, the broader the representation on the trips,
the more people that will be exposed to your country.

Thanks again.

Sincerely,

Roger A Keats
RSC

PHILIP M. CRANE
MEMBER OF CONGRESS
12TH DISTRICT, ILLINOIS

WAYS AND MEANS COMMITTEE
SUBCOMMITTEES:
HEALTH
SOCIAL SECURITY

Congress of the United States
House of Representatives
Washington, D.C. 20515

OFFICES:
SUITE 1406
LONGWORTH BUILDING
WASHINGTON, D.C. 20515
202/225-3711

SUITE 101
1450 SOUTH NEW WILKE ROAD
ARLINGTON HEIGHTS, ILLINOIS 60005
312/394-0790

June 10, 1975

C. P. Chang, First Secretary
Embassy of the Republic of China
2311 Massachusetts Avenue, N.W.
Washington, D.C. 20008

Dear C.P.:

Thank you for your generous hospitality and assistance while serving as escort for myself and other members of the Congressional Aide delegation which had an opportunity to visit the Republic of China as guests of the Pacific Cultural Foundation.

I thoroughly enjoyed all members of the group, though I must admit I often found myself in a distinct minority among so many of my liberal colleagues.

Your nation has an outstanding story of economic progress and defense of freedom which I thought was effectively told by the many meetings and excursions which were planned for us.

Also, thank you for taking the time to send a list of names to me of persons to whom I might wish to send a thank you letter for their hospitality.

After I have dug myself out of the considerable pile of work which accumulated during my absence from Washington, I look forward to having you as my guest for lunch at the Capitol Hill Club.

In the meantime, let me just reiterate that I hope you will feel free to call on me if I can be of any assistance to you. As you know, both Congressman Crane and I are strong supporters of your government.

Kind personal regards.

Cordially,

Richard S. Williamson
Administrative Assistant to
Philip M. Crane, M.C.

26

PHILIP M. CRANE
MEMBER OF CONGRESS
12TH DISTRICT, ILLINOIS

WAYS AND MEANS COMMITTEE
SUBCOMMITTEES:
HEALTH
SOCIAL SECURITY

Congress of the United States
House of Representatives
Washington, D.C. 20515

OFFICES:
SUITE 1406
LONGWORTH BUILDING
WASHINGTON, D.C. 20515
202/225-3711

SUITE 101
1450 SOUTH NEW WILKE ROAD
ARLINGTON HEIGHTS, ILLINOIS 60005
312/394-0790

July 7, 1975

Mr. C.P. Cheng, M.C.
The Republic of China
2311 Massachusetts Ave.
Washington, D.C.   20008

Dear C.P.:

I thoroughly enjoyed having the opportunity of visiting with you
and Victor over lunch at the Capitol Hill Club on Tuesday.

I will follow your suggestion and send a letter to Mr. Hu
giving an analysis and suggestions as a result of my trip to
the Republic of China.

As I mentioned to you at lunch, if there is any way in which I
can be of assistance to you, please never hesitate to contact me.

I am looking forward to dinner with you on July 11.

Kind personal regards.

Cordially,

Richard S. Williamson
Administrative Assistant to
Philip M. Crane, M.C.

RSW/ss

27

LLOYD BENTSEN
TEXAS

𝔘nited 𝔖tates 𝔖enate

WASHINGTON, D.C. 20510

27 August 1975

C.P.:

How can we ever thank you for what was a wonderful,
informative, exciting trip! It wouldn't have been
have as productive and useful for us if you had not
accompanied us and I mean that quite sincerely. You
understand the attitudes motivating the Congress,
you know how Americans think and act and react, and
you know an awfully lot about your own country -- put
those qualities together and they add up to a major
contribution to our visit. Plus your English, of
course, which is fantastic!

There is very little that I would change about the
trip -- I think it might be useful for future trips
to meet with private businessmen, for example, with
members of Taiwan's Chamber of Commerce. This would
be to discuss first-hand the problems that your
businessmen have had trading and investing abroad
or securing foreign investment in this country(Taiwan).
It also might be interesting to meet with labor
leaders about their efforts to influence government
decisions relating to the economy and labor conditions.
I might suggest as well meetings with newspaper people,
editorialists, reporters, etc. and perhaps with the
government's spokesman -- I sat next to him at dinner
at the Foreign Ministry and he was a particularly
intelligent and delightful gentleman.

As I mentioned, as soon as the McBrides return from
their travels, we want to invite you and your wife
to dinner some evening -- I certainly look forward to
meeting her and she is very lucky to have met you
before I did! It is my loss!!

One last word -- John Feng was particularly helpful
and knowledgeable for us -- I believe that was the
unanimous opinion of the group -- he seemed to understand American attitudes quite well as well as changing
perceptions of America's world role ---

Not Printed at Government Expense

Warm regards,

Lloyd

28

HERMAN E. TALMADGE, GA., CHAIRMAN

JAMES O. EASTLAND, MISS.   ROBERT DOLE, KANS.
GEORGE MC GOVERN, S. DAK.   MILTON R. YOUNG, N. DAK.
JAMES B. ALLEN, ALA.   CARL T. CURTIS, NEBR.
HUBERT H. HUMPHREY, MINN.   HENRY BELLMON, OKLA.
WALTER D. HUDDLESTON, KY.   JESSE HELMS, N.C.
DICK CLARK, IOWA
RICHARD B. STONE, FLA.
PATRICK J. LEAHY, VT.

MICHAEL R. MC LEOD
GENERAL COUNSEL AND STAFF DIRECTOR

United States Senate

COMMITTEE ON
AGRICULTURE AND FORESTRY
WASHINGTON, D.C. 20510

大使閣

下親啟

職光

主

現已自外交界退休。

台北擔任駐華大使館新聞專員，仍家殷懃諮詢，

B氏於一九五八一一九六二年間，曾在

September 4, 1975

Dear S. K:

That was an impressive trip to Taiwan. The changes were
tremendous. Once I got past the Embassy, USIS , JCRR, the
Presidential Palace and the Guest House, I was totally lost.
Chung Shan Bei Lu was unrecognizable.

C. P. was very good at herding us around. I don't think we
were really late for anything on the schedule.

I am preparing a report for the Senator on the trip. I have
already had a brief talk with him about it, but for the more
formal report, I want to check a few points with Joe Yager
with whom I have a lunch date. I talked on the phone to
Ambassador Drumright before I left and he told me he would be
out there too toward the end of last month, and also that Dave
Osborn would be in from Burma to visit him in California
before he and Florence took off.

You have done a great deal with that island. The Taichung
Harbor and the new shipyard in Kaohsiung are almost unbelievable.
I do think, however, that the Foundation ought to schedule a
briefing on social services for future visitors. As you know,
they are much in the news here in the States and I think
information about Taiwan's progress in this field would be
useful. I managed to get a hurried, special briefing on the
morning of the day we left.

Many thanks. The trip was a pleasure as well as being
informative.

Sincerely,

Bill

Charles W. Bergstrom
Legislative Aide to
Senator George McGovern

Minister S. K. Hu
Chinese Embassy
2311 Massachusetts Avenue, N. W.
Washington, D. C. 20008

29

RICHARD NOLAN
6TH DISTRICT, MINNESOTA

COMMITTEES:
AGRICULTURE
SMALL BUSINESS

JAMES A. DECHAINE
ADMINISTRATIVE ASSISTANT

1019 LONGWORTH HOUSE OFFICE BUILDING
WASHINGTON, D.C. 20515
(202) 225-2331

Congress of the United States
House of Representatives
Washington, D.C. 20515

September 17, 1975

Mr. C. P. Chang
Chinese Embassy
2311 Massachusetts Avenue, N. W.
Washington, D. C. 20008

Dear C.P:

I can't tell you how much I enjoyed seeing you and Cecilia on Monday evening at the Embassy. It was a fantastic evening and it was so nice to have an opportunity to renew old friendships.

C.P., I hope that we will all have an opportunity to get together again with you and your wife. Your friendship means a great deal to us and without your patience and assistance our trip would not have been so successful and enlightening.

Let me hear from you. Warmest personal regards.

Sincerely yours,

Sandy

SANDRA D. HANBURY

30

September 19, 1975

Dear Mr. Ambassador:

My wife Ann and I wish to thank you and Mrs. Shen very much for the marvelous dinner party at the Embassy on Monday. It was but another example of graciousness and hospitality which we are convinced is practiced by no one so well as by the people of Taiwan.

As I mentioned to you after dinner, I hope very much that your schedule and that of Senator Johnston will allow the two of you to get together for lunch some day soon here in the Capitol. I will discuss that possibility with C. P. and be back in touch with you later.

Again, our warmest thanks.

With kindest personal regards,

Sincerely,

Charles W. McBride

His Excellency James C. H. Shen
The Ambassador of China
Washington, D. C.

BCC: Mr. C. P. Chang

DAWSON MATHIS
SECOND DISTRICT
GEORGIA

October 2, 1975

Minister C. P. Chang
Embassy of the Republic of China
2311 Massachusetts Avenue
Washington, D. C. 20008

Dear Minister Chang:

On Thursday, October 9, I have the pleasure
of hosting a luncheon honoring Dr. Twanmou Kai,
Chairman of the Pacific Cultural Foundation in
Taiwan, Republic of China.

The luncheon will be at 12 noon at the
Democratic Club on New Jersey Avenue, S.E., and
I hope you will be able to attend and share this
time with Dr. Twanmou while he is in Washington.

Sincerely,

Dawson Mathis, M.C.

RSVP
Lex - 225-3631

PHILIP M. CRANE
MEMBER OF CONGRESS
12TH DISTRICT, ILLINOIS

WAYS AND MEANS COMMITTEE
SUBCOMMITTEES:
HEALTH
SOCIAL SECURITY

Congress of the United States
House of Representatives
Washington, D.C. 20515

OFFICES:
SUITE 1406
LONGWORTH BUILDING
WASHINGTON, D.C. 20515
202/225-3711

SUITE 101
1450 SOUTH NEW WILKE ROAD
ARLINGTON HEIGHTS, ILLINOIS 60005
312/394-0790

October 20, 1975

Mr. C. P. Cheng
Embassy
The Republic of China
2311 Massachusetts Avenue
Washington, D.C.   20510

Dear C.P.:

Both Jane and I enjoyed having a chance to visit with you
and Cecelia and so many of our other friends at the dinner
which Charlie McBride helped organize at the University Club on
October 9th. We saw Cecelia at the Chinese Embassy the following
night during the National Day celebration.

I hope you had an excellent "vacation" during the October
recess with the Senate group which you accompanied to Taiwan.

As you know, I hold you in the highest regard and appreciate
the occasional opportunities to visit with you.

Please find enclosed some photostats of various Congressional
Record statements that we made over the last few weeks pertaining
to the Republic of China which I think you might find of interest.
As you know, both Congressman Crane and myself are more than
happy to do whatever we can on behalf of the free people of the
Republic of China.

Kind personal regards.

Sincerely,

Richard S. Williamson
Administrative Assistant to
Philip M. Crane, M.C.

RSW/wss
Enclosures

33

RUSSELL B. LONG, LA., CHAIRMAN

HERMAN E. TALMADGE, GA.   CARL T. CURTIS, NEBR.
VANCE HARTKE, IND.   PAUL J. FANNIN, ARIZ.
ABRAHAM RIBICOFF, CONN.   CLIFFORD P. HANSEN, WYO.
HARRY F. BYRD, JR., VA.   ROBERT J. DOLE, KANS.
GAYLORD NELSON, WIS.   BOB PACKWOOD, OREG.
WALTER F. MONDALE, MINN.   WILLIAM V. ROTH, JR., DEL.
MIKE GRAVEL, ALASKA   BILL BROCK, TENN.
LLOYD BENTSEN, TEX.
WILLIAM D. HATHAWAY, MAINE
FLOYD K. HASKELL, COLO.

MICHAEL STERN, STAFF DIRECTOR
DONALD V. MOOREHEAD, CHIEF MINORITY COUNSEL

United States Senate

COMMITTEE ON FINANCE

WASHINGTON, D.C. 20510

October 22, 1975

Honorable C. P. Chang
First Secretary
Embassy of The Republic of China
Washington, D.C. 20008

Dear C.P.

A note of thanks for your hard work, patience and perseverance which made our trip to Taiwan a huge success.

This is the third such trip I have been on and by far this one was the most enjoyable.

Again, thank you for your gracious hospitality.

Best regards,

George W. Pritts

34

ABRAHAM RIBICOFF, CONN., CHAIRMAN

JOHN L. MC CLELLAN, ARK.   CHARLES H. PERCY, ILL.
HENRY M. JACKSON, WASH.   JACOB K. JAVITS, N.Y.
EDMUND S. MUSKIE, MAINE   WILLIAM V. ROTH, JR., DEL.
LEE METCALF, MONT.   BILL BROCK, TENN.
JAMES B. ALLEN, ALA.   LOWELL P. WEICKER, JR., CONN.
LAWTON CHILES, FLA.
SAM NUNN, GA.
JOHN GLENN, OHIO

RICHARD A. WEGMAN
CHIEF COUNSEL AND STAFF DIRECTOR

United States Senate

COMMITTEE ON
GOVERNMENT OPERATIONS
WASHINGTON, D.C. 20510

December 1, 1975

Mr. C.P. Chang
First Secretary
Office of the Embassy
Republic of China
2311 Massachusetts Avenue
Washington, D.C. 20008

Dear Mr. ~~Chang~~ *C.P.*,

At this time, as President Ford visits the PRC
I want to share my views with you on the subject of
Sino-American relations.

While it appears clear that the United States
will continue to strengthen its ties with the People's
Republic of China on the mainland, I believe it is most
important for the United States to remain a steadfast
and staunch friend of its loyal ally, the Republic of
China.

The friendship of our two peoples is a long one.
You have stood by us in time of war and peace and we have
developed a trading partnership which is beneficial to
both of our countries.

I hope that the United States will maintain this
friendship. Our mutual treaty obligations must remain
secure and our diplomatic and trading doors must remain
open.

I look forward to our continuing friendship and
I hope you will convey my thoughts to your colleagues,
all of whom have been most gracious and kind to me.

With very best wishes,

Sincerely,

Geoffrey G. Peterson
Administrative Assistant to
Senator Abe Ribicoff

PHILIP M. CRANE
MEMBER OF CONGRESS
12TH DISTRICT, ILLINOIS

WAYS AND MEANS COMMITTEE
SUBCOMMITTEES:
HEALTH
SOCIAL SECURITY

Congress of the United States
House of Representatives
Washington, D.C. 20515

OFFICES:
SUITE 1406
LONGWORTH BUILDING
WASHINGTON, D.C. 20515
202/225-3711

SUITE 101
1450 SOUTH NEW WILKE ROAD
ARLINGTON HEIGHTS, ILLINOIS 60005
312/394-0790

December 17, 1975

Mr. C. P. Cheng, M.C.
The Republic of China
2311 Massachusetts Avenue
Washington, D.C. 20008

Dear Mr. C. P.:

I enjoyed visiting with you at Roger Keats' farewell party
Thursday, December 4.

The next day I came across the article entitled "Taiwan's
remarkable allure for U.S. business," which appeared in the
December 15 issue of Business Week. From my visit in your
country, the commitment to the people and drive for indus-
trialization discussed in this article is certainly accurate.

I hope you and your family have an enjoyable holiday season.
After you return from your next "vacation" in Taiwan I hope
you will contact me, I would enjoy having lunch with you and
John.

Kind personal regards.

Cordially,

Rich

Richard S. Williamson
Administrative Assistant to
Philip M. Crane, M.C.

RSW/wab

36

January 5, 1976

Honorable C. P. Chang
First Secretary
Embassy of The Republic of China
Washington, D.C.   20008

Dear C.P.:

Many thanks for your thoughtful Christmas present.
The calendar has a reserved spot in my new office and
I hope you have an opportunity for a visit when you are
rested from your current trip.

In addition, let me take this opportunity to wish
you a happy and prosperous New Year.

Best regards,

George W. Pritts
Minority Counsel
Senate Finance Committee

PHILIP M. CRANE
MEMBER OF CONGRESS
12TH DISTRICT, ILLINOIS

WAYS AND MEANS COMMITTEE

SUBCOMMITTEES:
HEALTH
SOCIAL SECURITY

OFFICES:
SUITE 1406
LONGWORTH BUILDING
WASHINGTON, D.C. 20515
202/225-3711

SUITE 101
1450 SOUTH NEW WILKE ROAD
ARLINGTON HEIGHTS, ILLINOIS 60005
312/394-0790

Congress of the United States
House of Representatives
Washington, D.C. 20515

January 7, 1976

Mr. C. P. Cheng
Embassy of the Republic of China
2311 Massachusetts Avenue, N.W.
Washington, D.C. 20008

Dear C.P.:

Thank you for the delightful calendar from China
Airlines.

Both Jane and I hope that you and Cecillia had an enjoyable holiday season, and we wish you the best in the
New Year.

Cordially,

Richard S. Williamson
Administrative Assistant to
Philip M. Crane, M.C.

RSW/wab

38

HAROLD E. FORD
8TH DISTRICT, TENNESSEE

COMMITTEES:
BANKING, CURRENCY AND HOUSING
VETERANS' AFFAIRS
SELECT COMMITTEE ON AGING

WASHINGTON OFFICES:
1609 LONGWORTH HOUSE OFFICE BUILDING
WASHINGTON, D.C. 20515
(202) 225-3265

1430A LONGWORTH HOUSE OFFICE BUILDING
WASHINGTON, D.C. 20515
(202) 225-9215

H. A. GILLIAM, JR.
ADMINISTRATIVE ASSISTANT

Congress of the United States
House of Representatives
Washington, D.C. 20515

January 26, 1976

MEMPHIS OFFICES:
MAIN OFFICE:
369 FEDERAL BUILDING
MEMPHIS, TENNESSEE 38103
(901) 534-4131

SOUTH OFFICE:
1685 SOUTH LAUDERDALE
MEMPHIS, TENNESSEE 38106
(901) 534-4141

NORTH OFFICE:
1693 JACKSON
MEMPHIS, TENNESSEE 38107
(901) 534-4126

EAST OFFICE:
4515 POPLAR AVENUE
SUITE 418
MEMPHIS, TENNESSEE 38117
(901) 534-4129

WILLIE T. MILES
DISTRICT DIRECTOR

Mr. C. P. Chang
Embassy of the Republic of China
2311 Massachusetts Avenue N.W.
Washington, D.C.

Dear Mr. Chang:

I wish to express to you my sincere appreciation for the many courtesies extended to me during my recent visit to the Republic of China. The trip was a most enjoyable one, but more importantly, it was also a very enlightening exposure to the diplomatic, political, and social factors operative in the Far East.

One result of my exposure has certainly been a much deeper awareness of and sensitivity to the role, needs, and significance of the Republic of China. The enormous strides taken by the society of Taiwan in the last several years, in the face of an obviously imposing threat close to your shores, are most remarkable.

Even though your progress has been highly impressive, I believe the single most lasting impression I have is of the Chinese people themselves. Never have I been exposed to a more cohesive, industrious people. To me it is your spirit that ultimately augurs well for the success of your society.

There can be no question, in my mind, but that the United States, nor any other well-intentioned nation, cannot afford to overlook the Republic of China. While I do believe, as I have indicated, that initiatives with the mainland are proper and useful; to me there is no doubt that diplomatic recognition of Peking, to the exclusion of such recognition Taipei, would be most inappropriate.

I can truthfully say that this belief represents a shift in my previous thinking on this very delicate issue. Lack of exposure can be a distinct handicap to understanding, and I would encourage you to expose more of my peers to your nation and its aspiratons.

Again, I thank you for a most enjoyable trip and one which, beyond and above its pleasurable aspects, was a definite source of enlightenment.

Very sincerely,

H. A. GILLIAM, JR.
Administrative Assistant

HG:mo

39

HARRISON LOESCH
2440 VIRGINIA AVENUE, N. W.
APARTMENT D 905
WASHINGTON, D. C. 20037

February 6, 1976

The Honorable C. P. Chang
First Secretary
Chinese Embassy
2311 Massachusetts Avenue, N. W.
Washington, D. C.   20008

Dear C. P.:

For your information, I am attaching a copy of each of the letters
I have written to those on the list you suggested. I am very glad
you furnished it because I would surely have missed one or two if
you had not.

In addition to the letters, I have sent a specimen of reindeer horn
to eleven of them:

Mr. Chiang, Ching-kuo	Vice Admiral H. T. Wang
Dr. Joseph K. Twanmoh	Lt. General L. C. Kung
Dr. Tsai, Wei-ping	Lt. General C. L. Chiang
Mr. Sun, Yun-suan	Rear Admiral M. C. Chen
Mr. H. C. Yen	Governor T. M. Hsieh
Mr. C. O. Kuo	

Of course, I would be greatly remiss if I did not express my gratitude yet once more and in even stronger terms. That expression and
feeling belongs to you. From the initial lunch some weeks before we
went until the trip was over, one could see with half an eye that its
success was primarily due to your planning and executive ability.
I have never been on a trip where things went off so well, although
once in a while, of course, we had close calls. I am sure Charles
King was most disappointed when Herb showed up, for instance!

Louise and I were honored indeed to be invited to your home Chinese
New Year's Eve last week and enjoyed the evening tremendously. Louise,
who is no mean cook herself, was in ecstacy over the food and has re-
marked to a number of her friends how artistic the dishes were in addition to their taste. It was good to see John again, and I greatly
hope to arrange a small luncheon for both of you next week. If I can,
time will be so short I will have to invite you by telephone.

Thank you again for everything and please be assured that so far as I
am concerned, I am sure your objective on the trip was thoroughly
realized. Best personal regards and best wishes for the year of the
dragon.

Sincerely,

Harrison Loesch
Minority Counsel
Senate Committee on Interior and Insular
Affairs

HL:cs

ADMINISTRATIVE ASSISTANTS' ASSOCIATION
OF THE U.S. HOUSE OF REPRESENTATIVES

Room 2266 RHOB
Washington, D.C. 20515

February 16, 1976

The Honorable Chiang Ching-kuo
Premier, The Republic of China
Taipei, Taiwan
Republic of China

Dear Mr. Premier:

Recently I was privileged to visit the Republic of China and learn something of the dedication, accomplishments and valor of your people. Needless to say, I have never been so impressed in all of my other travels as I was with your nation.

In the midst of great adversity and with a seeming lack of great natural resources, you have carved out a land unmatched in the annals of time. We particularly appreciated the fact that you would allow us to visit with you personally, to pay our respects and to learn more about your great land. I was most impressed with the openness of your society and the genuine friendliness of your people. I was astounded at what you have been able to accomplish through drive and determination. I came with no particular credentials in mind, but I felt when I left that I had been among friends.

Let me digress to pay tribute to Mr. C. P. Chang of your Foreign Service. Here is a gentleman in whom any nation could feel justifiable pride. He is the most competent and dedicated Foreign Service official it has been my pleasure to meet and I value his friendship highly. He is a credit to you and to your great land and its people.

Again, my most sincere thanks for the opportunity to visit one of the great lands of this earth, one that I am confident will continue to prosper and which will continue to enjoy the friendship of the great majority of the people of these United States, its government and free men everywhere.

Sincerely,

HERB WADSWORTH
President

HW/cb

OFFICERS

Herb Wadsworth (Rep. Fuqua-Fla.)
President
Charles Holm (Rep. Ginn-Ga.)
Vice-President
Paul Stewart (Rep. Hinshaw-Calif.)
Vice-President
Mary Wood (Rep. Dingell-Mich.)
Secretary
Sherwood Boehlert (Rep. Mitchell-N.Y.)
Treasurer

REGIONAL DIRECTORS

Sid Hoyt (Rep. Devine-Ohio)
Thad S. Murray (Rep. Robt. Daniel-Va.)
Peter Ilchuk (Rep. Biaggi-N.Y.)
Eileen Nixon (Rep. Giaimo-Conn.)
Owen Chaffee (Rep. Leggett-Calif.)
Hank Sweitzer (Rep. Bevill-Ala.)
Jack Vance (Rep. Montgomery-Miss.)
George Berg (Rep. Hagedorn-Minn.)
Pete Scrivner (Rep. Price-Ill.)
George Eustaquio (Rep. Won Pat-Guam)

DIRECTORS-AT-LARGE

Dale Hulshizer (Rep. Evans-Col.)
Barbara Morris (Rep. Lent-N.Y.)
Charles Ward (Speaker Albert-Okla.)
Janet Watlington (Rep. De Lugo-V.I.)

PAST PRESIDENT

George Fisher (Rep. Teague-Tex.)

41

BOB BERGLAND
SEVENTH DISTRICT, MINNESOTA

WASHINGTON OFFICE:
1414 LONGWORTH HOB
WASHINGTON, D.C. 20515
TELEPHONE: (202) 225-2165

COMMITTEES:
AGRICULTURE
(CHAIRMAN, SUBCOMMITTEE ON
CONSERVATION AND CREDIT)
SMALL BUSINESS COMMITTEE

DISTRICT OFFICES:
IRENE MARING, SECRETARY
920 28TH AVENUE SOUTH
MOORHEAD, MINNESOTA 56560
TELEPHONE: (218) 236-5050

BOB KINSMAN, DISTRICT REP.
BOX 390
THIEF RIVER FALLS, MINNESOTA 56701
TELEPHONE: HOME (218) 681-4509

JACK DRESSEN, DISTRICT REP.
BROWERVILLE, MINNESOTA 56438
TELEPHONE: (612) 594-2738

CLIFF OUSE, DISTRICT REP.
ROTHSAY, MINNESOTA 56579
TELEPHONE (218) 867-2226

Congress of the United States
House of Representatives
Washington, D.C. 20515

February 24, 1976

Mr. C. P. Chang
Chinese Embassy
2311 Massachusetts Avenue
Washington, D. C. 20008

Dear C. P.:

I would like to recommend two excellent candidates for one of the future trips to Taiwan. Both are Administrative Assistants, both are relatively new here in Washington, D. C., and both are close personal friends to their Congressmen. Both Congressmen should be here for a long time and are rather liberal. As I stated in Taiwan, you need support from the liberal as well as the conservative element of the political system. Their names are Jim DeChaine, Congressman Richard Nolan's office, 225-2331 and Tom Reagan, Congressman James Oberstar's office, 225-6211. I highly recommend both and I think you would enjoy them on the trip.

Sincerely,

RON SCHRADER
Administrative Assistant to
Congressman Bob Bergland

RS:bes
p.s. I would appreciate it if you would send a letter asking for a short audience with Congressman Bergland to fill him in on some of the concerns you feel are important. Bring the Minister with you.

THIS STATIONERY PRINTED ON PAPER MADE WITH RECYCLED FIBERS

Congress of the United States
House of Representatives
Washington, D.C. 20515

February 27, 1976

Mr. C. P. Chang
First Secretary
Embassy of the Republic of China
2311 Massachusetts Avenue, N.W.
Washington, D. C. 20008

Dear C. P.:

There was an important omission on your list of
names for thank-you letters -- your own! More than anyone else, you bore the burden of work for the trip, and
we are more grateful than I can say for all you did.

Never in our lives have we learned so mush so fast!
In that short week we gained insight into the foreign
and domestic policies of your country; scratched the
surface of the great depth of Chinese culture; made
many new friends, and came to admire greatly the
Republic of China and its people.

We also came away with great admiration for your
talents, such as: going without sleep for days on end;
keeping track of twenty independent Americans, all trying to go off in different directions; taking seriously
and actually filling some of the most ridiculous requests
ever made (including steering Sara to City Park at six
o'clock in the morning!); drinking every toast while
showing no effects; and remaining your usual, good-
natured self in the face of what must have been extreme
provocation!

It's inadequate to say a mere "thank you", but there
just aren't any better words to express our gratitude
and admiration. So, a heartfelt thank-you, C. P.

One of the nicest elements of our visit was getting
to know you better. We are proud to count you a good
friend, and hope our friendship will continue for many,
many years.

With best wishes,

Cordially,

Sara M. Robinson
Counsel to
  Congressman Reuss

Donald L. Robinson
Chairman, Bi-Partisan
  Intern Committee

43

HERMAN E. TALMADGE, GA., CHAIRMAN

JAMES O. EASTLAND, MISS.   ROBERT DOLE, KANS.
GEORGE MC GOVERN, S. DAK.   MILTON R. YOUNG, N. DAK.
JAMES B. ALLEN, ALA.   CARL T. CURTIS, NEBR.
HUBERT H. HUMPHREY, MINN.   HENRY BELLMON, OKLA.
WALTER D. HUDDLESTON, KY.   JESSE HELMS, N.C.
DICK CLARK, IOWA
RICHARD B. STONE, FLA.
PATRICK J. LEAHY, VT.

MICHAEL R. MC LEOD
GENERAL COUNSEL AND STAFF DIRECTOR

United States Senate

COMMITTEE ON
AGRICULTURE AND FORESTRY
WASHINGTON, D.C. 20510

May 3, 1976

The Honorable C. P. Chang
Embassy of the Republic of China
2311 Massachusetts Ave., NW
Washington, D. C. 20008

Dear Mr. Chang:

I wish to take this opportunity to thank you for your personal part in arranging the Easter recess trip to the Republic of China, and to express my sincere gratitude for all the gracious hospitality toward our group.

It was a most impressive visit; I shall remember it with great affection for a long time to come.

With every good wish, I am

Sincerely,

JAMES C. WEBSTER
Chief Clerk

44

May 13, 1976

Dear C.P.:

This brief note will express my sincere appreciation for the many kindnesses and courtesies accorded the Congressional group who recently had the unique honor and privilege of visiting your beautiful country.

I speak for the entire group in thanking you specifically for your interest in making that wonderful opportunity possible. We were deeply impressed by all that we saw and learned during our stay in your homeland; and you may be assured we returned home with a strong feeling of affection and esteem for the people and the leaders of the Republic of China.

I, personally, hope to visit your country again, and the next time you organize a trip, I would like to recommend that you extend an invitation to Ms. Carolyn Smith, Administrative Assistant to the Honorable Shirley Chisholm, U.S. Congresswoman from New York.

With warmest regards, and, again, thank you.

Sincerely,

JANET B. WATLINGTON
Administrative Assistant

Mr. C.P. Chang
First Secretary
Embassy of the Republic of China
2311 Massachusetts Avenue, N.W.
Washington, D.C. 20008

ROBERT N. GIAIMO
THIRD DISTRICT, CONNECTICUT

WASHINGTON OFFICE:
2265 RAYBURN BUILDING
(202) 225-3661

DISTRICT OFFICE:
301 POST OFFICE BUILDING
NEW HAVEN, CONNECTICUT 06510
(203) 624-1308
(203) 432-2043
(203) 378-8410 (STRATFORD LINE)

ADMINISTRATIVE ASSISTANT
EILEEN NIXON

Congress of the United States
House of Representatives
Washington, D.C. 20515

May 26, 1976

COMMITTEE ON
APPROPRIATIONS

SUBCOMMITTEES:
DEPARTMENT OF DEFENSE
DISTRICT OF COLUMBIA
LEGISLATIVE BRANCH (CONGRESS)

COMMITTEE ON THE BUDGET

JOINT COMMITTEE ON
CONGRESSIONAL OPERATIONS

Mr. and Mrs. C. P. Chang
Embassy of the Republic of China
2311 Massachusetts Avenue
Washington, D.C. 20008

Dear C.P. and Mrs. Chang:

I cannot believe that so much time has lapsed since I had the pleasure of being in your home for dinner, and I hope you will forgive my tardiness in telling you how very much I enjoyed that lovely evening.

I have looked back on your dinner party with fond memories so many times, and I want to tell you how delightful the entire evening was. Only the hectic schedule which I have been keeping of late has prevented my putting my thoughts into writing.

It was so kind of you to have me and my colleagues into your home for the evening, and I know that each member of the group enjoyed the party as much as I did. Thank you again for your hospitality and kindness, and I do hope we'll have occasion to be together again soon.

Sincerely yours,

D. EILEEN NIXON
Administrative Assistant

DEN:sig

46

PHILIP M. CRANE
MEMBER OF CONGRESS
12TH DISTRICT, ILLINOIS

WAYS AND MEANS COMMITTEE
SUBCOMMITTEES:
HEALTH
SOCIAL SECURITY

OFFICES:
SUITE 1406
LONGWORTH BUILDING
WASHINGTON, D.C. 20515
202/225-3711

SUITE 101
1450 SOUTH NEW WILKE ROAD
ARLINGTON HEIGHTS, ILLINOIS 60005
312/394-0790

Congress of the United States
House of Representatives
Washington, D.C. 20515

June 4, 1976

Mr. C. P. Cheng
Embassy of the Republic of China
2311 Massachusetts Avenue, N.W.
Washington, D.C. 20008

Dear C.P.:

First let me express my deep appreciation for both Jane and myself for the lovely dinner which you and Cecil had earlier this month. We had a delightful time and as always your hospitality was boundless.

Thank you for sending me a copy of your letter to Terry Emerson with respect to the New York Times article on May 3, "Signs of Dissent Absent in Taiwan".

You made a persuasive and eloquent rebuttal to the distortions carried in the article. I am most impressed and appreciate you sharing these comments with me.

Kind personal regards.

Cordially,

Richard S. Williamson
Administrative Assistant to
Philip M. Crane, M.C.

RSW/wsb

47

PHILIP M. CRANE
MEMBER OF CONGRESS
12TH DISTRICT, ILLINOIS

WAYS AND MEANS COMMITTEE

SUBCOMMITTEES:
HEALTH
SOCIAL SECURITY

Congress of the United States
House of Representatives
Washington, D.C. 20515

OFFICES:
SUITE 1406
LONGWORTH BUILDING
WASHINGTON, D.C. 20515
202/225-3711

SUITE 101
1450 SOUTH NEW WILKE ROAD
ARLINGTON HEIGHTS, ILLINOIS 60005
312/394-0790

June 5, 1976

Mr. C.P. Cheng
Embassy of the Republic of China
2311 Massachusetts Avenue, N.W.
Washington, D.C.   20008

Dear C.P.:

I am in receipt of your note and the accompanying articles including
that by David Milton entitled "The New China Lobby is the Old China
Lobby".

I read David Miltons article with great interest. I believe the
statement he makes with respect to Dr. Schlessinger is correct to the
extent that Schlessinger seems to advocate a closer alignment with
Mainland China to counterbalance the potential threat of the Soviet
Union.

Mr. Milton's comment to the effect that "Taiwan hardly seems to matter
to them anymore," however, is way off point. It is my understanding
that Barry Goldwater continues to be a strong supporter of Taiwan.
Furthermore, we know from frequent contact that the Taiwan question is
of great importance to Governor Reagan.

I can only assure you that Congressman Crane's commitment to the
continued freedom of the Republic of China remains unaltered and that
his voice with Governor Reagan on this and other matters is significant.

Kind personal regards.

Cordially,

Richard S. Williamson
Administrative Assistant to
Philip M. Crane, M.C.

RSW/wsb

48

PHILIP M. CRANE
MEMBER OF CONGRESS
12TH DISTRICT, ILLINOIS

WAYS AND MEANS COMMITTEE

SUBCOMMITTEES:
HEALTH
SOCIAL SECURITY

OFFICES:
SUITE 1406
LONGWORTH BUILDING
WASHINGTON, D.C. 20515
202/225-3711

SUITE 101
1450 SOUTH NEW WILKE ROAD
ARLINGTON HEIGHTS, ILLINOIS 60005
312/394-0790

Congress of the United States
House of Representatives
Washington, D.C. 20515

July 20, 1976

Mr. C. P. Cheng
Embassy of the Republic of China
2311 Massachusetts Avenue, N.W.
Washington, D.C. 20008

Dear C.P.:

I think you will find the enclosed correspondence of interest.

Thanks for all your help on my brief stay in the Republic of China.

Let's get together for lunch soon.

Kind personal regards.

Cordially,

Richard S. Williamson
Administrative Assistant to
Philip M. Crane, M.C.

RSW/wab

Enclosure:

49

HOUSE OF REPRESENTATIVES
WASHINGTON, D. C. 20515

J. KENNETH ROBINSON
SEVENTH DISTRICT
VIRGINIA

September 14, 1976

Dear C. P. -

   I hope by now you have recooperated fully from jet lag and that you are feeling quite yourself again. The last of my boxes arrived from Taiwan the day before yesterday, and everything is accounted for and in good shape.

   I just want to personally thank you for the opportunity of being invited on the visit as a member of the Congressional Staff Delegation. It was a wonderful experience and one that I will never forget, you can be sure!

   Enclosed is a copy of the letter I wrote to Dr. Twanmoh for your information. The names and addresses you provided were most helpful, and the last letter from the list was posted this morning.

   I really feel I learned a great deal from the trip - a fact David noticed when he and I discussed the trip over a Chinese dinner soon after my return. So you see, it was worth-while for me, and I am now in the process of getting a report together for Mr. Robinson.

   Please give my best to Cecilia and Michele.

   In gratitude, I am

                              Sincerely yours,

                              Pam

                              Pamela Dale Snyder

Mr. Chang Chia-piao
First Secretary
Embassy of the Republic of China   P.S. Looking forward to
2311 Massachusetts Avenue, N. W.   seeing you on
Washington, D. C. 20008   the 24th/

RALPH H. METCALFE
First District, Illinois

COMMITTEES:
INTERSTATE AND
FOREIGN COMMERCE
MERCHANT MARINE AND
FISHERIES
CHAIRMAN:
SUBCOMMITTEE ON
PANAMA CANAL
MEMBER:
DEMOCRATIC STEERING AND
POLICY COMMITTEE

WASHINGTON OFFICE:
322 Cannon Building
PHONE: (202) 225-4372

DISTRICT OFFICES:
230 S. Dearborn Street
Room 3846
Chicago, Illinois 60604
PHONE: (312) 353-4105

454 E. 79th Street
Chicago Illinois 60619
PHONE: (312) 651-4200

Congress of the United States
House of Representatives
Washington, D.C. 20515

October 7, 1976

Mr. C. P. Chang
Embassy of the Republic of China
2311 Massachusetts Avenue, N. W.
Washington, D. C. 20008

Dear C. P.:

Enclosed please find a copy of 'U. S.
Foreign Policy: Principles for Defining the
National Interest". The section that I referred
to is on page 48. However, I think you will find
the entire report interesting.

With every best wish.

Sincerely,

Coleman J. Conroy
Legislative Assistant

Enclosure

CJC:ama

*Looking forward to seeing you
& Larry at dinner next Wednesday.
Kay will be joining us & two other
individuals whom I referred to in
our last conversation*

51

𝒰nited States Senate
WASHINGTON, D.C.

October 29, 1976

Mr. C.P. Chang
First Secretary
Chinese Embassy
2311 Massachusetts Avenue, N.W.
Washington, D.C. 20008

Dear C.P.:

A good friend of mine, Dan Minchew, is one of Jimmy Carter's
advisors on international trade issues. He is a Georgian and
a member of the International Trade Commission. He was the
Administrative Assistant to Senator Talmadge before joining
the I.T.C.

Last week, Dan spoke to the Federal Bar Association on Carter's
views on international trade. I thought you might want to read
his remarks and pass them along to whomever reviews this in the
embassy, or to send it back home to people following this in
the foreign ministry.

In addition, Dan had spoken earlier this year in Georgia about
the need for a Department of International Trade. If Carter
wins the election, I expect Dan will play a role in his administration in the trade area, and I would not be surprised to see
this speech as one blueprint for Carter's government reorganiza-
tion. Thus, I think it should be of interest to you and your
colleagues.

I indicated to Dan that I had some friends in embassies here
who would enjoy reading his remarks, and he sent me copies of
both speeches. I hope they are of interest to you and your
colleagues.

Best regards.

Sincerely,

Walt Evans
Legal Counsel to
Senator Mark O. Hatfield

WE:jl

RON DE LUGO
DELEGATE, VIRGIN ISLANDS

COMMITTEE ON INTERIOR
AND INSULAR AFFAIRS

SUBCOMMITTEES:
TERRITORIAL AND INSULAR AFFAIRS
NATIONAL PARKS AND RECREATION
ENVIRONMENT
INDIAN AFFAIRS

Congress of the United States
House of Representatives
Washington, D.C. 20515

1217 LONGWORTH BUILDING
WASHINGTON, D.C. 20515
(202) 225-1790

P.O. BOX 65
7 KING CROSS STREET
CHRISTIANSTED, ST. CROIX
(809) 773-5900

22 CRYSTAL GADE
CHARLOTTE AMALIE, ST. THOMAS
(809) 774-4408

January 5, 1977

RDCG: 01577

Mr. C. P. Chang
First Secretary
Embassy of the Republic of China
2311 Massachusetts Avenue, N. W.
Washington, D. C. 20008

Dear C. P.:

Congressman deLugo has requested that I forward the attached letter to you for your review and consideration.

I would appreciate your furnishing Mr. Knowlton with the information he requests.

Thank you for your courtesy.

With warmest personal regards. I am looking forward to our meeting again soon.

Sincerely,

JANET B. WATLINGTON
Administrative Assistant

January 18, 1977

Mr. Richard Moe
3611 Underwood Street
Chevy Chase, MD   20015

Dear Dick:

Please accept my heartiest congratulations and best wishes on your appointment as the Chief of Staff to the Vice President of the United States of which I was delighted to learn from today's Washington Post.

I sincerely believe that Vice President-elect Walter F. Mondale couldn't have made a better choice in choosing you as his top aide in the light of his future role as an active Vice President in the new administration; and I also ardently hope that you will, as a witness of our striving for progress and survival, exert whatever influence you can toward stimulating a greater understanding of the aspirations of the government and people of the Republic of China on Taiwan.

Enclosed for your reference is a copy of Chairman Thomas E. Morgan's report to the House Committee on International Relations on a factfinding mission to the Far East in November, 1976.

With warmest personal regards to you and Julia.

Sincerely yours,

C. P. Chang
First Secretary

54

OFFICE OF THE VICE PRESIDENT

WASHINGTON

January 27, 1977

Mr. C. P. Chang
First Secretary
Embassy of the Republic of China
2311 Massachusetts Avenue, N. W.
Washington, D. C. 20008

Dear C. P.:

Thanks so much for your kind note. I deeply appreciate it and it was very thoughtful of you to write.

We are just getting settled in here, as you can imagine, but, so far, things are coming along very nicely. Needless to say, we are all excited about the prospects that lie ahead.

I appreciate your thoughtfulness in forwarding me a copy of Chairman Morgan's report to the House Committee on International Relations on a factfinding mission to the Far East. I look forward to reading it.

Many thanks again and my warmest regards.

Sincerely,

Richard Moe
Chief of Staff

Embassy of the Republic of China
2311 Massachusetts Avenue, N.W.
Washington, D.C. 20008

February 3, 1977

Mr. Richard Moe
Chief of Staff to the Vice President
The White House
Washington, D.C. 20500

Dear Dick:

Recently, I have received several copies of an "urgent press conference invitation" released by a so-called "Taiwaness Rights and Culture Association" from my friends in Congress who wanted to know the truth about the alleged kidnapping of a Mr. Hsing-nan Wang by my government.

To straighten the facts, I am sending you as enclosed a copy of the "press conference invitation" and a copy of news release from Taipei for your perusal. If you have any more doubt, please check the State Department for confirmation.

The real victim of this case, my friend, is our beloved Governor Hsieh of the Taiwan Provincial Government whose left hand was blown off by a letter bomb engineered and mailed by Wang who was convicted, through due process of law, for his taking terrorist action against the government officials.

The terrorist group, organized abroad, has engaged in activities against its own country from the shelter of a foreign land--the United States. And whenever their terrorist or subversive activities were uncovered and thence arrests were made, they would grasp such opportunity to discredit my government by launching an organized and massive media campaign in the name of "human right."

The terrorists will strike again in the future and their organization in the U.S. will continue to poison the American public with their ungrounded venomed attack on my government. As our two nations are progressing through a very difficult period in our history, I urge you to help us explaining to Vice President Mondale the true nature of this case.

Sincerely,

C. P. Chang
First Secretary

OFFICE OF THE VICE PRESIDENT

WASHINGTON

February 24, 1977

`. C. P. Chang
.rst Secretary
bassy of the Republic of China
11 Massachusetts Avenue, Northwest
shington, D.C.   20008

ar Mr. ~~Chang~~ C. P.:

I wanted to thank you for your letter regarding Mr. Wang Hsing-nan and the incident which resulted in injury to Governor Hsieh.

In response to my inquiries, the Department of State has informed me that the Federal Bureau of Investigation is looking into the charges that individuals in the United States were involved in the parcel bomb case.

I want to assure you that the Administration deplores terrorists acts such as the one that injured Governor Hsieh and that we are determined to take every appropriate step to halt the spread of international terrorism.

Sincerely,

Richard Moe
Chief of Staff

LARRY GOLDWATER
ARIZONA

𝔘𝔫𝔦𝔱𝔢𝔡 𝔖𝔱𝔞𝔱𝔢𝔰 𝔖𝔢𝔫𝔞𝔱𝔢

WASHINGTON, D.C. 20510

February 3, 1977

Mr. C. P. Chang
First Secretary
Embassy of the Republic of China
2311 Massachusetts Avenue, N.W.
Washington, D. C.   20008

Dear C.P:

Thank you very much for your prompt action in sending our office background information relative to the
accusation that Wang Hsing-nan was kidnapped and im-
properly sentenced by your government. It is very
important that your friends be able to respond immediately to false charges of this kind and if you had
not been so prompt in supplying us with information, we
would have been completely in the dark about the matter.

As you know, there is a new emphasis in America upon
morality and human rights in connection with the shaping
and carrying out of foreign policy. One of the strong
arguments against weakening U.S. ties with the Republic
of China is the sharp contrast between adherence to law
by your government and the total lack of decency or
law in the Communist government on the Mainland. Thus,
whenever a single charge is made against your government
that would smear it as being lawless, it is vital to
relations between our countries that strong answers be
provided as soon as possible.

Thanks to your swift action, our office was alerted to
the press criticism and we are prepared to answer it.
In fact, Senator Goldwater is working on a speech to
turn the propaganda of the terrorist group around against
them by showing that this very case demonstrates the fact
that rule by law prevails in the Republic of China.

59

The very fact that Mr. Wang could travel so freely into
and out of Taiwan reveals the freedom of travel that no
ordinary person on the Mainland enjoys. The fact that
he was entitled to have a defense attorney at his trial
and to be tried openly, with press and relatives in
attendance, all demonstrate that principles of justice
are followed by your government. And, the fact that
Mr. Wang has a right of appeal of his sentence is further
proof of the operation of law in your society.

We would like to present details of the trial process,
such as the above, in the form of a speech so that the
American public can see that even a defendant accused
of the terrible crime of terrorism resulting in human
injury is given rights under the law. It would be
helpful to us if you would continue to collect material
concerning the trial and in particular, provide us with
answers to the new charges that have been made claiming
that Mr. Wang's face was bruised after his arrest. I
would like to discuss this subject further with you in
a few days.

Sincerely,

J. Terry Emerson
Legislative Assistant
    to U.S. Senator Barry Goldwater

𝔘𝔫𝔦𝔱𝔢𝔡 𝔖𝔱𝔞𝔱𝔢𝔰 𝔖𝔢𝔫𝔞𝔱𝔢

WASHINGTON, D.C. 20510

December 9, 1977

His Excellency
James C. H. Shen
Ambassador of the Republic of China
Embassy of the Republic of China
2311 Massachusetts Avenue, N.W.
Washington, D.C. 20008

Dear Mr. Ambassador:

I appreciate your kind note of December 2, 1977
in reply to my letter to you of November 29 concerning
my interest in Florida citrus imports into Taiwan.

In connection with my upcoming trip to the Republic
of China, it would be helpful to me if Mr. C. P. Chang
of your staff might be available in Taipei during that
time. Mr. Chang and John Feng of your staff have been
extremely helpful to me in preparing my itinerary. To
the extent that would be appropriate, his continued
assistance while I am in Taiwan would be beneficial, to
both myself and to Bill Pursley and Roy Werner, the staff
assistants who are accompanying me.

Wishing you and yours a happy holiday season.

Most cordially,

Richard (Dick) Stone

RDS/bpj

61

RICHARD (DICK) STONE
FLORIDA

COMMITTEES:

AGRICULTURE, NUTRITION, AND
FORESTRY
FOREIGN RELATIONS
VETERANS' AFFAIRS

United States Senate

WASHINGTON, D.C. 20510

January 24, 1978

Mr. C. P. Chang
Embassy of the Republic of China
2311 Massachusetts Avenue, N.W.
Washington, D.C. 20008

Dear CP:

This is to express my great appreciation for all you did to make our visit to the Republic of China such an outstanding success.

Your advice and counsel, both in planning our trip and during the trip, were of immeasurable value. In addition, Marlene and I will never forget your many kindnesses and special attention while we were in Taiwan.

I look forward to a continuing association over the years to come and hope you will be able to visit us in our Tallahassee home in the near future.

Warm personal regards.

Sincerely,

Richard (Dick) Stone

RDS/bpj

62

WALTER D. HUDDLESTON
KENTUCKY

COMMITTEES:
AGRICULTURE AND FORESTRY
APPROPRIATIONS
SELECT COMMITTEE ON
INTELLIGENCE

United States Senate

WASHINGTON, D.C. 20510

March 1, 1978

The Honorable C. P. Chang
Counselor
Embassy of the Republic of China
2311 Massachusetts Avenue, N.W.
Washington, D. C. 20008

Dear C. P.:

I have just learned that you are soon to retire from
your position as Counselor for the Embassy of the Republic of China and that you will be entering private business with a firm in Taiwan. I view this with mixed emotions. We will certainly miss you here in Washington
and I know that the Embassy will find your position difficult to fill. I know, however, from what you have
told me that you are looking forward to new challenges
and I suspect that your future will be as successful as
your past has been.

As I understand it, your new position as Vice President of the Chung Hwa Boat Company will keep you in the
United States a good part of the time. Although most of
your work will have you on the west coast, I hope that
from time to time you will be able to visit Washington.
When you are in the city, please be sure to stop by my
office.

As a United States Senator, I have had many, many
occasions to deal with diplomats from foreign Embassies.
I can honestly say, however, that I have never had the
pleasure of associating with a more gracious and competent person than C. P. Chang.

You have my warmest wishes for the greatest success
in your new endeavor. Please give my regards to Cecilia.

Sincerely,

Walter D. Huddleston

63

JOHN SPARKMAN, ALA., CHAIRMAN

FRANK CHURCH, IDAHO
CLAIBORNE PELL, R.I.
GEORGE MC GOVERN, S. DAK.
HUBERT H. HUMPHREY, MINN.
DICK CLARK, IOWA
JOSEPH R. BIDEN, JR., DEL.
JOHN GLENN, OHIO
RICHARD (DICK) STONE, FLA.
PAUL S. SARBANES, MD.

CLIFFORD P. CASE, N.J.
JACOB K. JAVITS, N.Y.
JAMES B. PEARSON, KANS.
CHARLES H. PERCY, ILL.
ROBERT P. GRIFFIN, MICH.
HOWARD H. BAKER, JR., TENN.

NORVILL JONES, CHIEF OF STAFF
ABNER E. KENDRICK, CHIEF CLERK

United States Senate

COMMITTEE ON FOREIGN RELATIONS

WASHINGTON, D.C. 20510

March 2, 1978

Honorable C. P. Chang
Counselor
Embassy of the Republic of China
2311 Massachusetts Avenue, N.W.
Washington, D.C. 20008

Dear C.P.:

I enclose an autographed photograph.

As you know, it has been a pleasure to work with you in your Embassy connection. I am sorry that you are leaving Washington. Let me wish you all success in your new venture.

Sincerely,

John Sparkman

Enclosure

64

UNITED STATES SENATE

WASHINGTON, D. C. 20510

JOHN GLENN
OHIO

March 2, 1978

Dear C. P.:

It is with regret that I learn of your coming
retirement from the Foreign Service. You have been
an excellent representative of your government, and
you have done an outstanding job of furthering the
positions and interests of the Republic of China.

You have been of great assistance to me and
my staff in working with the issues affecting our
countries, and you will certainly be missed. I
hope we have an opportunity to see each other in
the future.

Best of luck on your new endeavor. I am confident you will do well.

Best regards.

Sincerely,

John Glenn
United States Senator

Mr. C. P. Chang
Counselor
Embassy of the Republic of China
2311 Massachusetts Avenue, Northwest
Washington, D. C. 20008

United States Senate
WASHINGTON, D.C.

March 2, 1978

The Honorable C. P. Chang
Counselor
EMBASSY OF THE REPUBLIC OF CHINA
2311 Massachusetts Avenue, N. W.
Washington, D. C. 20008

My dear C. P.:

It was with profound regret that I learned
from Rogers of your imminent retirement. You
will certainly be missed by all of us whom you
leave behind.

The deep and lasting friendships which you have
made, both personally and professionally, will
last for many, many years to come. I know that
you must feel a deep sense of satisfaction for
the important role that you have played in
strengthening the ties of cooperation and friendship between the Republic of China and the
United States. Our two nations will profit by
your hard work as they move through this difficult period of history.

Please let me know whenever we can be of service,
and again, thank you for your friendship and
cooperation through the years.

With best wishes, and kindest personal regards,
I am

Sincerely,

Herman E. Talmadge

DEPARTMENT OF STATE

Washington, D.C. 20520

March 2, 1978

Mr. Chia-piao Chang
Counselor
Embassy of the
  Republic of China
2311 Massachusetts Avenue, N.W.
Washington, D. C.   20008

Dear C. P.:

Thank you for your kind letter of
February 28. I am sorry to hear that
you will be leaving Washington soon --
yes, let's keep in touch. I hope that
your business on Taiwan will prosper
and that it will bring you much happiness.

                    Best,

                              Sincerely,

C.P. -- I've
so enjoyed
our friendship -
you & Cecilia
have meant a lot to me -- I
don't want to lose touch
will think of you
often --
    Love, S.

                              Sally A. Shelton
                              Deputy Assistant Secretary
                              for Inter-American Affairs

67

DONALD J. MITCHELL
31st District, New York

COMMITTEES:
ARMED SERVICES
SUBCOMMITTEE ON
MILITARY INSTALLATIONS
RANKING MINORITY MEMBER
SUBCOMMITTEE ON
MILITARY COMPENSATION
ASSISTANT REGIONAL WHIP

Congress of the United States
House of Representatives
Washington, D.C. 20515

1527 Longworth House
Office Building
Washington, D.C. 20515
Telephone (202) 225-3665

DISTRICT OFFICES:
319 North Main Street
Herkimer, New York 13350
(315) 866-1051

100 West Main Street
Johnstown, New York 12095
(518) 762-4508

200 Church Street
Rome, New York 13440
(315) 339-0013
(Mon-Wed-Fri)

6 Steuben Park
Utica, New York 13501
(315) 724-9302

March 3, 1978

Hon. C.P. Chang, Counselor
Embassy of the Republic of China
2311 Massachusetts Avenue, N.W.
Washington, D.C. 20008

Dear C.P.:

It was with mixed emotions that I received your announcement about your future plans.

Of course I was excited for you when I learned of your new venture and in this and in all things for the future I wish you the very best.

However, I must confess disappointment over the fact that a good and true friend will soon be so far away. You'll be missed. It's my sincere hope your travels and mine will permit frequent occasions for get-togethers.

I'm also a little sad to see the Embassy lose such an able and articulate spokesman at a time when so much is at stake for the Republic of China in your country's relationship within the family of nations. Never, in my 14 years in Washington, have I come across a diplomat who measures up to you in terms of dedication and talent.

I know, as I'm sure the leaders of your government know, C.P. Chang is someone who can be counted on . Quite frankly, there's no doubt in my mind that you will always be there when needed. I don't think the diplomatic corps has seen the last of C.P. Chang.

As you depart, do so knowing in your heart that you leave behind so very many friends who value your friendship, respect your integrity, admire you for your dedication and ability and wish for you good health, much happiness and all the best in life.

Sincerely,

Sherwood L. Boehlert
Executive Assistant

SLB:b

68

WARREN G. MAGNUSON, WASH., CHAIRMAN

HOWARD W. CANNON, NEV.	JAMES B. PEARSON, KANS.
RUSSELL B. LONG, LA.	ROBERT P. GRIFFIN, MICH.
ERNEST F. HOLLINGS, S.C.	TED STEVENS, ALASKA
DANIEL K. INOUYE, HAWAII	BARRY GOLDWATER, ARIZ.
ADLAI E. STEVENSON, ILL.	BOB PACKWOOD, OREG.
WENDELL H. FORD, KY.	HARRISON H. SCHMITT, N. MEX.
JOHN A. DURKIN, N.H.	JOHN C. DANFORTH, MO.
EDWARD ZORINSKY, NEBR.	
DONALD W. RIEGLE, JR., MICH.	
JOHN MELCHER, MONT.	

United States Senate

COMMITTEE ON COMMERCE, SCIENCE,
AND TRANSPORTATION

WASHINGTON, D.C. 20510

March 3, 1978

Mr. C. P. Chang
First Secretary
Embassy of the Republic of China
2311 Massachusetts Avenue, N.W.
Washington, D. C.   20008

Dear C.P.:

I have just learned of your plan to retire from the Foreign Service in the immediate future. I sincerely hope you will enjoy great success in your future enterprise, although I regret very much having to lose the presence of a trusted and valued friend and professional colleague.

Since first meeting you in 1974, I have enjoyed and relied upon our working relationship and the close friendship which soon developed. I have rarely met anyone of any nationality of your ability, energy, integrity and loyalty to your Country and convictions.

There are many qualities which I could remark upon that helped to deepen my respect for, and friendship with you, but just to mention a few, there is the broad scope of your knowledge, your patience, your understanding of the needs of others, and your boundless energy.

But both as a friend and an associate, I thank you for never failing to provide me with prompt and reliable information that Senator Goldwater and I might have requested in connection with one or another issue involving the Republic of China. Your information always held up, which strengthened our position and gave us confidence.

Again, I wish you the greatest of success for the future and hope that our friendship will be renewed in the future.

Sincerely,

J. Terry Emerson
Counsel to U.S. Senator Barry Goldwater

69

ADMINISTRATIVE ASSISTANTS ASSOCIATION
U.S. HOUSE OF REPRESENTATIVES

Room 2207 RHOB
Washington, D.C. 20515

March 3, 1978

Honorable C. P. Chang
Counselor
Embassy of the Republic of China
2311 Massachusetts Avenue, N.W.
Washington, D. C. 20008

Dear C. P.:

My best wishes go with you as you leave the Foreign Service of the
Republic of China and undertake private business ventures.

It has been my pleasure to know you during your service in Washington,
and our acquaintance has broadened my perspective on the problems and the
ideals of the people of the Republic of China. Certainly you have made a
fine contribution to your government and your people through your service
in Washington, and you are to be commended for the dedication and competence
which you brought to your position.

I wish you a safe journey, and I hope you will keep in touch whenever
you are in this area.

Best wishes to you for every happiness and good fortune in all your
undertakings, C. P.

Sincerely yours,

Eileen

EILEEN NIXON
President

OFFICERS

Eileen Nixon (Rep. Giaimo — Conn.) 秀十四姊七助理
President
William T. Deitz (Rep. Thompson — N.J.)
Vice President
Thas S. Murray (Rep. Daniel — Va.)
Vice President
Herb Wadsworth (Rep. Fuqua — Fla.) 秀十四姊七助理
Secretary
George Eustaquio (Rep. Won Pat — Guam)
Treasurer

REGIONAL DIRECTORS

Ivan "Red" Swift (Rep. Perkins — Ky.)
Marguerite Furfari (Rep. Staggers — W.Va.)
Dave Lovenheim (Rep. Horton — N.Y.)
Tim Sullivan (Rep. Howard — N.J.)
Jim Cousins (Rep. Patterson — Calif.)
Walter J. Pittman (Rep. Fountain — N.C.)
Sharon Matts (Rep. Brooks — Tex.)
Ray Lancaster (Rep. Jones — Tenn.)
Randall Robinson (Rep. Diggs — Mich.)
Bill Robertson (Rep. Ullman — Oreg.)

DIRECTORS-AT-LARGE

David L. Batt (Rep. Waggonner — La.)
Keith Hall (Rep. Quie — Minn.)
Gary Madson (Rep. Leach — Ia.)
Bette Welch (Rep. Pease — Ohio)

PAST PRESIDENTS

George Fisher (Rep. Teague — Tex.)
Herb Wadsworth (Rep. Fuqua — Fla.) 秀十四姊七助理
Charles R. Holm, Jr. (Rep. Ginn — Ga.) 秀十- 姊七助理
Sherwood L. Boehlert (Rep. Mitchell — N.Y.) 洋五姊七助理

HOWARD W. CANNON, NEV., CHAIRMAN

WARREN G. MAGNUSON, WASH.	JAMES B. PEARSON, KAN.
RUSSELL B. LONG, LA.	ROBERT P. GRIFFIN, MICH.
ERNEST F. HOLLINGS, S.C.	TED STEVENS, ALASKA
DANIEL K. INOUYE, HAWAII	BARRY GOLDWATER, ARIZ.
ADLAI E. STEVENSON, ILL.	BOB PACKWOOD, OREG.
WENDELL H. FORD, KY.	HARRISON H. SCHMITT, N. MEX.
JOHN A. DURKIN, N.H.	JOHN C. DANFORTH, MO.
EDWARD ZORINSKY, NEBR.	
DONALD W. RIEGLE, JR., MICH.	

AUBREY L. SARVIS, STAFF DIRECTOR AND CHIEF COUNSEL
EDWIN K. HALL, GENERAL COUNSEL
MALCOLM M. B. STERRETT, MINORITY STAFF DIRECTOR

United States Senate

COMMITTEE ON COMMERCE, SCIENCE,
AND TRANSPORTATION
WASHINGTON, D.C. 20510

March 3, 1978

Mr. C. P. Chang, Vice President
Chung Hwa Boat Building Company, Limited
8th Floor, Number 27, Pao Ching Road
Taipei, Taiwan
Republic of China

Dear C. P.:

Although I'm writing this letter to you before your
date of departure to Taipei, I think it will reach
you there long before I have a chance to see you here.

I want you to know as you leave for home that you leave
behind you a host of admirers and people who appreciate
the great work you have done for your country in the
United States. I wish you the very best of happiness
and success in the future; and now that I know someone
in the boat building business, if I ever get a dime
ahead, I may call on you.

A photograph is going to you under separate cover.

With best wishes,

Barry Goldwater

March 6, 1978

C.P. Chang, Counselor
Embassy of the Republic of China
2311 Massachusetts Avenue, N.W.
Washington, D.C. 20008

Dear C.P.:

Just a note to tell you how much we're going to miss you here in Washington. I know how much you have been looking forward to returning to Taipei and I was delighted to hear that you have secured a wonderful position there and that you may also be going into the consulting business. I have no doubt that you would be very successful in both but particularly the latter since you understand our country so well. You have my very best wishes and I hope you'll keep in touch.

By all means, let me know whenever you get back to the States.

Warmest regards.

Sincerely,

Richard Moe
Chief of Staff

72

HERMAN E. TALMADGE, GA., CHAIRMAN

JAMES O. EASTLAND, MISS.	BOB DOLE, KANS.
GEORGE MC GOVERN, S. DAK.	MILTON R. YOUNG, N. DAK.
JAMES B. ALLEN, ALA.	CARL T. CURTIS, NEBR.
WALTER D. HUDDLESTON, KY.	HENRY BELLMON, OKLA.
DICK CLARK, IOWA	JESSE HELMS, N.C.
RICHARD B. STONE, FLA.	S. I. HAYAKAWA, CALIF.
PATRICK J. LEAHY, VT.	RICHARD G. LUGAR, IND.
EDWARD ZORINSKY, NEBR.	
JOHN MELCHER, MONT.	
KANEASTER HODGES, JR., ARK.	

MICHAEL R. MC LEOD
GENERAL COUNSEL AND STAFF DIRECTOR

United States Senate

COMMITTEE ON
AGRICULTURE, NUTRITION, AND FORESTRY
WASHINGTON, D.C. 20510

March 6, 1978

Mr. C. P. Chang
Counselor
Embassy of the Republic of China
2311 Massachusetts Avenue, N. W.
Washington, D. C. 20008

Dear C. P.:

It is with deep regret and best wishes that I contemplate your leaving the Foreign Service to enter private business in Taiwan.

It has certainly been a pleasure to have known you these last two years and I hope to continue to see you in your new occupation. I will always have fond memories of my trip to Taiwan and your wonderful hospitality as our host. I believe that you have made a real and lasting contribution to better relations between the people in the United States and the people of the Republic of China.

I am confident that you will be successful in your new occupation for I know you will bring the same enthusiasm and good cheer to this job that you have always exhibited in the Foreign Service.

With best wishes and warmest personal regards, I am

Sincerely,

MICHAEL R. McLEOD
General Counsel and
Staff Director

73

JAMES O. EASTLAND
MISSISSIPPI

PRESIDENT PRO TEMPORE

United States Senate

WASHINGTON, D.C. 20510

March 8, 1978

The Honorable C. P. Chang
Counselor
Embassy of the Republic of China
2311 Massachusetts Avenue, N. W.
Washington, D. C.   20008

Dear Counselor Chang:

I was happy to learn that you plan to go home to the Republic of China to enter what I know will be a very successful business enterprise.

On the other hand, I am sorry that your great country will be without the services of a dedicated, talented and effective diplomatic representative.

As you depart from Washington, you take with you my warmest best wishes for a full measure of health and happiness.

With kindest regards,

Sincerely,

James Eastland

James O. Eastland
President Pro Tempore

JOE:sm

HOWARD H. BAKER, JR.
TENNESSEE

𝕌nited States Senate
WASHINGTON, D.C. 20510

March 8, 1978

Mr. C. P. Chang
Counselor
Embassy of the Republic of China
2311 Massachusetts Avenue, N. W.
Washington, D. C. 20008

Dear C. P.:

I just wanted to take this opportunity to wish you well
in your new endeavors as you return to Taiwan.

Your efforts in behalf of your countrymen have been in
the finest tradition of public service. I know your
many friends in Washington join me in wishing you much
continuing success and happiness.

Sincerely,

Howard H. Baker, Jr.

HHBJr:alh

Enclosure

Congress of the United States
House of Representatives
Office of the Majority Leader
Washington, D.C. 20515

March 8, 1978

Hon. C. P. Chang, Counselor
Embassy of the Republic of China
2311 Massachusetts Avenue, NW
Washington, DC   20008

Dear C. P.:

Marshall tells me that you will be leaving Washington soon to join a very prestigious yacht building company in Taiwan. You will be sorely missed in Washington, my friend.

Even though I haven't been able to spend as much time with you as I would have preferred, I am familiar with the fine work you have done here as a representative of the Republic of China. You and your people have a great story to tell, and you have been a truly eloquent spokesman.

I understand that your new enterprise will be bringing you often to the United States. Please consider this letter as a standing invitation to you to drop by the office anytime you are in town, and whenever my staff or I can be of assistance to you in any way.

Enclosed you will find an autographed picture. I hope you will accept it as a memento of our friendship.

With best wishes,

Sincerely,

Jim Wright

Enclosure

JOHN SPARKMAN, ALA., CHAIRMAN

FRANK CHURCH, IDAHO
CLAIBORNE PELL, R.I.
GEORGE MC GOVERN, S. DAK.
DICK CLARK, IOWA
JOSEPH R. BIDEN, JR., DEL.
JOHN GLENN, OHIO
RICHARD (DICK) STONE, FLA.
PAUL S. SARBANES, MD.
MURIEL HUMPHREY, MINN.

CLIFFORD P. CASE, N.J.
JACOB K. JAVITS, N.Y.
JAMES B. PEARSON, KANS.
CHARLES H. PERCY, ILL.
ROBERT P. GRIFFIN, MICH.
HOWARD H. BAKER, JR., TENN.

NORVILL JONES, CHIEF OF STAFF
ABNER E. KENDRICK, CHIEF CLERK

United States Senate

COMMITTEE ON FOREIGN RELATIONS

WASHINGTON, D.C. 20510

March 8, 1978

P E R S O N A L

Mr. C. P. Chang
Counselor, Embassy of
 the Republic of China
2311 Massachusetts Avenue, N. W.
Washington, D. C. 20008

Dear C. P.:

On the eve of your retirement from the Foreign Service, I
simply wanted to add my personal appreciation for your assistance
during the last few years and wish you the very best of luck in
your new career. I can think of no other representative of a
government who has so ably presented his nation's case in the Halls
of Congress.

I have found my contact with you to be both informative and
enjoyable -- one cannot ask for more than that combination. Your
skills are such that one can easily imagine you as an official of the
T'ang Dynasty. I shall certainly miss your prompt, incisive answers to
my queries and your willingness to teach me as we speculated upon possible scenarios regarding diplomatic events in East Asia.

If I can be of assistance to you or your family in the future,
please do not hesitate to call on me. Likewise, I trust that simply
because you are starting a second career, this does not mean we shall
not see one another in the future.

With all best wishes,

Cordially yours,

Roy A. Werner
Professional Staff Member

77

RUSSELL B. LONG, LA., CHAIRMAN

HERMAN E. TALMADGE, GA.   CARL T. CURTIS, NEBR.
ABRAHAM RIBICOFF, CONN.   CLIFFORD P. HANSEN, WYO.
HARRY F. BYRD, JR., VA.   ROBERT J. DOLE, KANS.
GAYLORD NELSON, WIS.   BOB PACKWOOD, OREG.
MIKE GRAVEL, ALASKA   WILLIAM V. ROTH, JR., DEL.
LLOYD BENTSEN, TEX.   PAUL LAXALT, NEV.
WILLIAM D. HATHAWAY, MAINE   JOHN C. DANFORTH, MO.
FLOYD K. HASKELL, COLO.
SPARK M. MATSUNAGA, HAWAII
DANIEL PATRICK MOYNIHAN, N.Y.

MICHAEL STERN, STAFF DIRECTOR
GEORGE W. PRITTS, JR., MINORITY COUNSEL

United States Senate

COMMITTEE ON FINANCE

WASHINGTON, D.C. 20510

March 9, 1978

Mr. C. P. Chang
Counselor
Embassy of the Republic of China
2311 Massachusetts Avenue, N. W.
Washington, D. C. 20008

Dear Mr. Chang:

As your tour of duty in Washington draws to a close, I want to thank you for all you have done to help me better understand the Republic of China and its relations with the United States and the world.

I have had the pleasure of spending many hours with you in Washington and Taiwan discussing a wide range of subjects. I have never failed to be impressed by your broad grasp of American and international politics, American and Chinese culture, and human nature. Your friendship has not only educated me--it has enriched my life. I know you have had this same effect on the many other American friends you have made.

I wish you the best of success in your new venture. I am sure you will continue to do excellent work in meeting this new challenge.

Sincerely,

Michael Stern

Michael Stern
Staff Director

78

ROBERT N. GIAIMO, CONN.
CHAIRMAN

JIM WRIGHT, TEX.
THOMAS L. ASHLEY, OHIO
ROBERT L. LEGGETT, CALIF.
PARREN MITCHELL, MD.
OMAR BURLESON, TEX.
LOUIS STOKES, OHIO
ELIZABETH HOLTZMAN, N.Y.
BUTLER DERRICK, S.C.
OTIS PIKE, N.Y.
DONALD FRASER, MINN.
DAVID R. OBEY, WIS.
WILLIAM LEHMAN, FLA.
PAUL SIMON, ILL.
JOSEPH L. FISHER, VA.
NORMAN Y. MINETA, CALIF.
JIM MATTOX, TEX.

GEORGE GROSS,
EXECUTIVE DIRECTOR
225-7200

DELBERT L. LATTA, OHIO
JAMES T. BROYHILL, N.C.
BARBER B. CONABLE, JR., N.Y.
MARJORIE S. HOLT, MD.
JOHN H. ROUSSELOT, CALIF.
JOHN J. DUNCAN, TENN.
CLAIR W. BURGENER, CALIF.
RALPH S. REGULA, OHIO

WILLIAM LILLEY III,
MINORITY STAFF DIRECTOR

NINETY-FIFTH CONGRESS

U.S. House of Representatives
COMMITTEE ON THE BUDGET
Washington, D.C. 20515

March 13, 1978

C. P. Chang, Counselor
Embassy of the Republic of China
2311 Massachusetts Avenue, N.W.
Washington, D.C. 20008

Dear C. P.:

Thank you so much for your letter about your retirement from the Foreign Service and your future plans in private business.

You have been an outstanding representative of your country, and I know the Foreign Service as well as your many friends in Washington will miss you. You can, indeed, feel a sense of pride in your many contributions toward strengthening the ties of understanding between our two countries.

I want to thank you personally for your many kindnesses to me and for your friendship. I wish you every success in your new venture. I hope we can stay in touch.

Best personal regards,

Jack McDonald
Special Assistant to the Chairman

79

United States Senate
WASHINGTON, D. C. 20510

RICHARD (DICK) STONE
FLORIDA

March 14, 1978

Dear C.P.:

All your friends will miss you here.

On the other hand, I am sure you will
have a great career ahead in the Republic of
China. We are confident that you will maintain
the excellent relations with the United States
which you played such an instrumental part in
fostering here.

Marlene and I so much appreciated the
arrangements you made for us on our visit to
Taipei, and we hope to see you there again
very soon.

Best of luck to you.

Warm personal regards.

Most cordially,

80

March 14, 1978

Mr. C. P. Chang
Vice President
Chung Hwa Boat Building Co., Ltd.
8th Floor, No. 27, Pao Ching Road
Taipei, Taiwan
Republic of China

Dear C.P.:

Congratulations on your appointment as Vice President of the Chung Hwa Boat Building Company. I know that your great energy, intelligence, and dedication will insure your success in business in the same manner as these attributes made you so effective as a representative of your government in Washington.

It has been a joy for Pearl and me to know you and Cecilia as friends. We will miss you both, and we are saddened by your departure. But this sorrow is alleviated by the enthusiasm you so obviously have for the challenge presented by your new career in the world of business and by the knowledge that your duties will bring you regularly to the United States and, hopefully, to Washington to visit the many friends you have made here.

In my six years of service as a Staff person in the U.S. House of Representatives, I met many people representing a broad variety of interests. No one I met during these years more effectively represented his cause than you. Not only are you a persuasive advocate, C.P., you are a man who wins the respect and admiration of those with whom you work because of your deep patriotism, your belief in your country and its future. More than that, you won our friendship because you so obviously cared about us, members of Congress and staff, as people, and were so understanding of and sensitive to our problems. We will all remember you and Cecilia for the time and hospitality you extended to us on so many occasions.

-2-

I don't want this letter to say goodbye, for I
hope to continue to see you in your new position. But
I couldn't let you leave without this expression of
appreciation and friendship. Thanks, C.P., and good
luck.

Sincerely,

George A. Dalley
Deputy Assistant Secretary
for International
Organization Affairs

March 15, 1978

Dear C.P.,

The news that you are leaving the Embassy and the United
States is very sad -- I have enjoyed our association very
much throughout these years. However, I know you have
a great opportunity ahead of you and I am sure you will
have continued success in your new endeavors.

With as many friends and colleagues both in and out of
our government as you have you can be assured of
assistance or support if ever you should need it. But
please call on us if there is anything I can do for you.

I wish you all the best in your new position -- your
company is indeed fortunate to have you, and I hope I
shall see you in Taipei -- or in Washington, soon.

My best,

Lisbeth K. Godley
Deputy Assistant Secretary for
Administrative and Legislative
Policy

Mr. C.P. Chang
Vice President
Chung Hwa Boat Building Co., Ltd.
8th Floor, No. 27, Pao Ching Road
Taipei, Taiwan
Republic of China

DEPARTMENT OF THE TREASURY
WASHINGTON, D.C. 20220

March 20, 1978

Dear C.P.:

It is with great regret that I learn of your decision to retire from Foreign Service and leave Washington, D.C.

You have been an invaluable friend and of great service in increasing the communication and understanding between our two countries. You have been of immense assistance to me and have demonstrated a unique capability of personal friendship and official representation.

I am hopeful that your decision to return to Taipei will not diminish our close friendship nor the opportunity to see you.

Sincerely,

Gene E. Godley
Assistant Secretary
(Legislative Affairs)

Mr. C. P. Chang
Vice President
Chung Hwa Boat Building Co., Ltd.
8th Floor, No. 27, Pao Ching Road
Taipei, Taiwan
Republic of China

DEPARTMENT OF HOUSING AND URBAN DEVELOPMENT
JOHN F. KENNEDY FEDERAL BUILDING
BOSTON, MASSACHUSETTS 02203

REGION I

March 20, 1978   IN REPLY REFER TO:

C. P. Chang
Vice President
Chung Hwa Boat Building Co., Ltd.
8th Floor, No. 27, Pao Ching Road
Taipei, Taiwan
Republic of China

Dear C.P.:

In your premature retirement from government service,
I want to wish you all the excitement, interest, and
enrichment a new career can bring.

Getting to know you was a refreshing experience and a
warm friendship which I am confident will continue into
private life.

My only regret is not being able to personally escort
you throughout New England and explain my own version of
the events which helped to create the United States 300
years ago. I am sure that you would have been told that
the Irish were responsible for every success and every
victory!

I am grateful that C. P. Chang and his family, and his
friends, happened to cross my path several years ago.
And, again, my deepest appreciation for all your many
kindnesses, and the hope that you will continue to stay
in touch with me, even though Pao Ching Road is a long
way from Boston Common.

My very best wishes.

Sincerely,

Edward T. Martin
Regional Administrator

85

JOHN SPARKMAN, ALA., CHAIRMAN

FRANK CHURCH, IDAHO
CLAIBORNE PELL, R.I.
GEORGE MC GOVERN, S. DAK.
HUBERT H. HUMPHREY, MINN.
DICK CLARK, IOWA
JOSEPH R. BIDEN, JR., DEL.
JOHN GLENN, OHIO
RICHARD (DICK) STONE, FLA.
PAUL S. SARBANES, MD.

CLIFFORD P. CASE, N.J.
JACOB K. JAVITS, N.Y.
JAMES B. PEARSON, KANS.
CHARLES H. PERCY, ILL.
ROBERT P. GRIFFIN, MICH.
HOWARD H. BAKER, JR., TENN.

NORVILL JONES, CHIEF OF STAFF
ARTHUR M. KUHL, CHIEF CLERK

United States Senate

COMMITTEE ON FOREIGN RELATIONS

WASHINGTON, D.C. 20510

March 21, 1978

Mr. C. P. Chang, Counselor
Embassy of the Republic of China
2311 Massachusetts Avenue, N.W.
Washington, D. C. 20008

Dear C. P.:

Although I deeply regret the reason for the event, it was
awfully good to see you at the party prior to your departure.
As you know, the ties between the United States and the
Republic of China transcend any personal relationships, but
I am certain that your presence in Washington has made that
relationship stronger than it would have been without you.

Completely apart from my responsibilities for the Senator, I
value our friendship because for me it is a continuation of
a personal alliance with the Republic that began in 1967
during what was to be the first of many port visits to
Kaohsiung.

Both Sally and I wish you the best of luck in the boat business and hope that it brings you back to Washington very
frequently. Keep in touch, and if there is anything I can
do for Cecilia in your absence, please do not hesitate to let
me know.

Sincerely,

G. Cranwell Montgomery
Legislative Assistant to
SENATOR HOWARD H. BAKER, JR.

GCM:gh

86

2266 RAYBURN HOUSE OFFICE BUILDING
WASHINGTON, D.C. 20515

CONGRESS OF THE UNITED STATES
HOUSE OF REPRESENTATIVES
WASHINGTON, D.C. 20515

March 22, 1978

Mr. C. P. Chang
Counselor
Embassy of the Republic of China
2311 Massachusetts Avenue, N. W.
Washington, D. C. 20008

Dear C. P.:

The enclosed photograph is sent with my very best wishes for every success in the future.

You have certainly represented your nation and its people both wisely
and well and your contribution to the development of this great country
will ever be remembered by those who cherish devotion, honor and sacri-
fice which you have exemplified.

Our prayers go with you and your family.

Sincerely,

DON FUQUA
Member of Congress

DF:mw
Enclosure

CHICAGO MERCANTILE EXCHANGE
International Monetary Market   Associate Mercantile Market

1629 K Street N.W. Washington, DC 20006 202/223-6673

April 3, 1978

C. Dayle Henington
Vice President
Government Relations

Mr. C. P. Chang
Vice President
Chung Hwa Boat Building Co., Ltr.
8th Floor, No. 27, Pao Ching Road
Taipei, Taiwan, R.O.C.

Dear C.P.:

Although we continue to have some difficulty accepting your departure
from the Washington scene, we trust that your new association in Taipei
will afford future opportunities for us to be together. As for your
former associates, both at the Embassy and in the Foreign Ministry at
home, I know they will miss your wise counsel on so many matters.
Certainly, those of us in Washington could always count on your views
being filled with great insight, even on the most complex issues.

On so many occasions, I have expressed my opinion regarding the service
you rendered to the Republic of China in this way. No country represented in the United States had a more able, dynamic, and wise representative here. Your many friends involved in our government, as I
was with Congressman W. R. Poage when he was Chairman of the Committee
on Agriculture of the House of Representatives, were always impressed
with your knowledge and understanding of our own issues. It was nothing
less than outstanding and, of course, made it possible for you to ad-
vise your own government of the complexities (or the simplicities) which
dictated a particular action or policy. In this entire area of congressional and government relations, you performed superbly, always maintaining the trust of all of us who were priveleged to work with you.

With every good wish for your future, I am

Sincerely your friend,

88

RICHARD (DICK) STONE
FLORIDA

COMMITTEES:
AGRICULTURE, NUTRITION, AND
FORESTRY
FOREIGN RELATIONS
VETERANS' AFFAIRS

United States Senate

WASHINGTON, D.C. 20510

April 20, 1978

Mr. C. P. Chang
Department of North American Affairs
Ministry of Foreign Affairs
Taipei, Taiwan
Republic of China

Dear C.P.:

Many thanks for the excellent efforts
you provided in helping the Florida Citrus
Commission people to consummate the first
sale of Florida citrus to the Republic of
China. All of us in Florida are most
appreciative.

Hope to see you real soon, either here or
in Taipei.

Warm personal regards.

Sincerely,

Richard (Dick) Stone

RDS/wep

89

JOHN SPARKMAN, ALA., CHAIRMAN

FRANK CHURCH, IDAHO
CLAIBORNE PELL, R.I.
GEORGE MC GOVERN, S. DAK.
DICK CLARK, IOWA
JOSEPH R. BIDEN, JR., DEL.
JOHN GLENN, OHIO
RICHARD (DICK) STONE, FLA.
PAUL S. SARBANES, MD.
MURIEL HUMPHREY, MINN.

CLIFFORD P. CASE, N.J.
JACOB K. JAVITS, N.Y.
JAMES B. PEARSON, KANS.
CHARLES H. PERCY, ILL.
ROBERT P. GRIFFIN, MICH.
HOWARD H. BAKER, JR., TENN.

NORVILL JONES, CHIEF OF STAFF
ABNER E. KENDRICK, CHIEF CLERK

United States Senate

COMMITTEE ON FOREIGN RELATIONS
WASHINGTON, D.C. 20510

May 24, 1978

Mr. C. P. Chang
Chung Hwa Boat Building Co., Ltd.
Eighth Floor, 27 Pao Ching Road
Taipei, Taiwan 100

Dear C. P:

Thank you very much for your recent letter. I have been wondering how you have been finding your "freedom" from government responsibilities. Is it true that the private sector demands more effort and more time?

I appreciate your kind words regarding my assistance to you, but would point out, as you know all too well, that it was two-way traffic and mutually beneficial. I, too, am pleased that our paths have crossed and trust that they will continue to do so in the years ahead.

I will be discussing your comments with Bill regarding representation of Ohio products in Taiwan. Frankly, this is an area in which I am a total novice and I presume that Bill, with his legal background, will be the primary source of advice to both the Senator and constituents.

I insist you make time for me on your schedule in this country in June and look forward to discussing your impressions of the business community and your role therein. I trust this finds you well and soon to be reunited with your family.

With best regards,

Yours cordially,

Roy A. Werner
Professional Staff Member

P. S. I see that your new business is worth $28 million per year with 80% of the exports coming to the United States.

90

United States Senate

WASHINGTON, D.C. 20510

July 14, 1978

His Excellency Yun-Suan Sun
Premier
Taipei, Taiwan
REPUBLIC OF CHINA

Dear Mr. Premier:

I want to take this opportunity to thank you for
your personal assistance in arranging the recent
purchases of Florida citrus products by the Republic
of China Central Trust. These purchases have made a
considerable impact in Florida and represent the
beginning of what I hope will be a growing trade
relationship between Florida and the Republic of China.

I know that Florida's citrus industry is anxious to
further develop commercial relations with the Republic
of China next year and in the years to come. I look
forward to working with you and your government,
assisting in such developments in any appropriate way.

All kind regards.

Most cordially,

Richard (Dick) Stone

RDS/wep

cc: The Honorable K.S. Chang, Minister of Economic Affairs
    Mr. H. K. Shao, Director General, Board of Foreign Trade
    Mr. C. P. Chang

91

BARRY GOLDWATER
ARIZONA

COMMITTEES:

ARMED SERVICES
   TACTICAL AIR POWER SUBCOMMITTEE
   INTELLIGENCE SUBCOMMITTEE
   RESEARCH AND DEVELOPMENT SUBCOMMITTEE
COMMERCE, SCIENCE AND TRANSPORTATION
   SCIENCE, TECHNOLOGY AND SPACE
   AVIATION
   COMMUNICATIONS
SELECT COMMITTEE ON INTELLIGENCE
   VICE CHAIRMAN

United States Senate

WASHINGTON, D.C. 20510

July 26, 1978

Mr. C. P. Chang

Dear C. P.:

John Feng said he would have this letter delivered to you
because you had moved and he didn't know your current address.

A very close, personal friend of mine, whom I've known and
worked with for many, many years, Dr. Ronald Nairn of
Scottsdale, Arizona, and his wife, Mona, will be visiting
Taipei, arriving August the 31st on China Airlines 2. They
will be staying at the Grand Hotel and will depart on September the 3rd on China Airlines Flt. 601.

Ron has been most instrumental and helpful to me in my work
and speech writing on the Republic of China. In fact, he
has been my inspiration and has kept me on the right path.
He is the most knowledgeable man I know on Southeast Asia,
and I know you will really like him.

As a personal favor to me, it would be greatly appreciated
if you could visit with him and assist him in his needs while
in Taipei. He will be there on business and would like to
chat with you about what he is doing, so anything you can
do would mean a lot to me.

I'm dictating this to Judy and she says hello, as do I, and
I hope one of these days you will return to the United States,
if only for a visit, so we can renew acquaintance.

With best wishes,

Barry Goldwater

92

OFFICE OF THE PREMIER
REPUBLIC OF CHINA

August 7, 1978

The Honorable Richard Stone
United States Senate
Washington, D.C. 20510
U. S. A.

Dear Senator Stone:

I wish to thank you for your letter of July 14, 1978 regarding the first sales of Florida citrus products to the Republic of China. It is my pleasure to inform you that the Central Trust of China has recently directed its representative in San Francisco to conclude an agreement with one of the Florida exporters for the purchase of US$1.1 million orange juice.

Please be assured that my government will continue to purchase Florida citrus fruits in the years to come with a view to helping promote the name and taste of Florida citrus products in Taiwan. I will instruct Mr. H.K. Shao, Director General, Board of Foreign Trade to work closely with Florida Citrus Department regarding next year's purchase. We are very sincere in our commitment to develop trade relationship between the Republic of China and Florida.

On the recent U.S. Senate's adoption of the Dole-Stone Amendment which expressed the sense of Senate in urging the Administration to consult with the Senate before making any changes in the 24-year-old mutual defense treaty with the Republic of China, I want to extend you the heartfelt appreciation of myself and the Chinese people in consponsoring this very important document in the annals of Sino-American relations.

We are greatly encouraged that this is the first time that the U.S. Senate has unanimously approved an amendment related to a mutual defense treaty in order to stress its importance. The significance of the vote indicates that the Republic of China has friends in the United States and particular her Senate.

With warmest personal regards,

Sincerely yours,

Y.S. Sun
Premier

cc: Minister C.H. Shen, MOFA
Ambassador James Shen, Chinese Embassy in Washington
Minister K.S. Chang, MOEA
Minister C.C. Chang, MOF
Mr. S.C. Liu, CTC
Mr. H.K. Shao, Board of Foreign Trade
Mr. C.P. Chang

United States Senate

WASHINGTON, D.C. 20510

COMMITTEES:

ARMED SERVICES
TACTICAL AIR POWER SUBCOMMITTEE
INTELLIGENCE SUBCOMMITTEE
RESEARCH AND DEVELOPMENT SUBCOMMITTEE
COMMERCE, SCIENCE AND TRANSPORTATION
SCIENCE, TECHNOLOGY AND SPACE
AVIATION
COMMUNICATIONS
SELECT COMMITTEE ON INTELLIGENCE
VICE CHAIRMAN

August 22, 1978

Mr. C. P. Chang
President
C. P. Chang & Company
D-2, 9th Floor
309 Tun-Hwa N. Road
Taipei, Taiwan
Republic of China

Dear C. P.:

Thanks for your letter of the 4th and I have made a copy of it
and have sent it on to Ron Nairn. You are so nice to meet these
fine people at the airport and assist them.

Relative to the other two paragraphs of your letter, you may be
sure that I will do everything within my power to keep our relations
with Taiwan as they are, that is, full recognition.

I showed your letter to Judy and Terry and they both send their
best wishes and we all hope to see you here in the United States
one of these days.

Again, thank you for your courtesies to the Nairns.

With best wishes,

Barry Goldwater

JOHN SPARKMAN, ALA., CHAIRMAN

FRANK CHURCH, IDAHO   CLIFFORD P. CASE, N.J.
CLAIBORNE PELL, R.I.   JACOB K. JAVITS, N.Y.
GEORGE MC GOVERN, S. DAK. JAMES B. PEARSON, KANS.
HUBERT H. HUMPHREY, MINN. CHARLES H. PERCY, ILL.
DICK CLARK, IOWA   ROBERT P. GRIFFIN, MICH.
JOSEPH R. BIDEN, JR., DEL. HOWARD H. BAKER, JR., TENN.
JOHN GLENN, OHIO
RICHARD (DICK) STONE, FLA.
PAUL S. SARBANES, MD.

NORVILL JONES, CHIEF OF STAFF
ABNER E. KENDRICK, CHIEF CLERK

United States Senate

COMMITTEE ON FOREIGN RELATIONS

WASHINGTON, D.C. 20510

October 28, 1978

Mr. C. P. Chang
D-2, 9th Floor
309, Tun-Hwa N. Rd.
Taipei, Taiwan
The Republic of China

Dear Mr. Chang:

Thank you for your gracious letter and your kind comments regarding my office. I trust you are enjoying your return home and finding your new business profitable and enjoyable.

I do hope to visit Taiwan during my next trip to northeast Asia. However, I have set no dates for such a trip. Of course, I have frequently been in and out of Taiwan during my career as an international businessman, and I am quite familiar with the prosperity of the Republic of China. Obviously, such a trip would provide an opportunity to discuss important items with the leadership of the Republic of China, and I look forward to such an exchange of views.

Best regards,

Sincerely,

John Glenn
United States Senator

JG/rwa

華美企業 / 寰球股份有限公司
HWA MEI INTERNATIONAL DEVELOPMENT INC.
4TH FL. 610 TUN HWA S. RD. TAIPEI TAIWAN R. O. C.
TEL.7089640 · 7054331~9 TELEX 19028 HWAMEITW

Mr. Richard Moe
Chief of Staff
Office of the Vice President
The White House
Washington, D.C. 20500
U. S. A.   June 19, 1979

Dear Dick:

     When President Carter announced the shocking news
of breaking official tie with the Republic of China on
Taiwan, I was surprised but not shocked. On the other
hand, I felt profoundly sad that this great nation's
power and influence were indeed declining.

     Later on, when Communist China's No.2 man Teng
Hsiao-Ping visited America, I was dismayed but rather
amused to see on TV the unseemly red carpet treatment
extended to Teng by the President of the United States.
Nevertheless, given the euphoria of that period of time,
I really shouldn't blame the poor protocal officer for
overacting.

     But now, when I each day pass the Taipei Office of
American Institute in Taiwan, I feel pained in seeing
the long lines waiting patiently, under the scorching sun
or thundering rain of the merciless and notorious Taipei
summer, for their turn to get an appointment number for
an interview at a God-knows-when date in order to obtain
a visa. And most of these people are only applying for a
non-emigration visa to visit the U.S. to see their loved
one, to pursue advanced study, or simply to do business.

     Upon checking, I have learned that it now takes more
than a month to get a visa for a visit to the U.S. The
journey of pilgrimage is of the following sequence:

     1. You stand in line averaging 4-6 hours for obtaining
visa application forms and a calling number for an unspe-
cified date of appointment for the visa interview.

中華民國台北市敦化南路610號(科普大厦4樓)電話：7089640 · 7054331~9

97

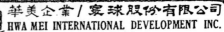
   2. You wait for 3-4 weeks to receive the notification
of your appointment date from the newspaper announcement.

   3. After the interview, you wait, crossing your
fingers, for another week or so to learn whether or not
you are granted a visa.

   4. If not, you can't argue with the Taipei Office of
AIT or even ask the reason for being refused a visa,
because AIT is a non-governmental private corporation
acting on behalf of U.S. Consulate General in Hong Kong.

   I am enclosing a copy of AIT's notice for your
reference and I call this document the greatest achieve
ment in legal technicality that was ever made in the history
of mankind. And I am wondering how far these whiz kids in
your administration's foreign affairs side -- who made
their debut in the wake of the trauma of Vietnam War --
can go in consummating their ardent desire of getting rid
of all the Asian allies and friends of the United States
during the previous administrations.

   It is extremely difficult to know the standards by
which to measure whether a great nation's power and
influence are declining. But I would be misleading you
if I did not report that there is a deep sense of unease
in Asia (I travelled extensively in Southeast Asia and
Middle East in recent months) about the direction of
America's foreign policy. There is no doubt that not only
U.S. prestige but major U.S. interests are being openly
questioned and challenged.

   More significant, perhaps, is the doubt that is
growing about whether it is worthwhile to be a friend of
the United States, whether it may not be actually dangerous
to be a friend of the United States -- as the fate of far
too many countries shows only too clearly. Senator Moyniham
couldn't have been more right when he said that the U.S. now
has "so few allies, and so many of them are slipping into
almost irreversible patterns of appeasement based on the
assumption that American power is invariably declining."

華美企業 / 寰球股份有限公司
HWA MEI INTERNATIONAL DEVELOPMENT INC.
4TH FL. 610 TUN HWA S. RD. TAIPEI TAIWAN R. O. C.
TEL 7089640 · 7054331~9 TELEX 19028 HWA MEITW

It may seem presumptuous for a non American to discuss with you the U.S. foreign policy, but I had lived seven and half years, out of my twenty-six years of working life, in Washington, D.C. and have a deep affection for it, for its nation and its people. Therefore it pained me to see that this great nation is now degenerating into using legal technicality to avoid the responsibility of properly treating "the people on Taiwan" when they apply an U.S. visa.

The United States may treat us as second class world citizens, but no one dares to deny that we are a nation of gallant people who have made this part of China the richest, the most modern and democratic place that China has ever seen throughout its five-thousand years of history.

One belittles oneself when one tries to belittle one's old friend.

With warmest personal regards,

Sincerely,

C. P. Chang
President

C.P. Chang, President
Hwa Mei International Development, Inc.
4th Floor, 610 Tun Hwa S. Rd.
Taipei, Taiwan R.O.C.

Dear C.P.:

Thanks so much for your letter. I was dis-
tressed to learn that there is such a delay in
obtaining visas in Taipei to travel to the U.S.
I can certainly understand your feelings about
this matter, and am inquiring to see what can be
done about it. If I should receive any encouraging
news, by all means I'll get back to you.

In the meantime, I hope all's well. Hope to
see you soon.

With warmest regards,

Sincerely,

Richard Moe
Chief of Staff

中華民國台北市敦化南路610號(村肯大厦4樓)電話：7083640・7054331～9

華美企業 / 寰球股份有限公司
HWA MEI INTERNATIONAL DEVELOPMENT INC.
4TH FL 610 TUN HWA S. RD. TAIPEI TAIWAN R. O. C.
TEL 7089640 · 7054331~9 TELEX 19028 HWA MEITW

Mr. Richard Moe
Chief of Staff
Office of the Vice President
The White House
Washington, D.C.20500
U. S. A.   July 17, 1979

Dear Dick:

    Thank you for your letter of July 9, 1979. It was
most thoughtful of you to write me and assure me of your
concern about my feelings towards AIT.

    I am sending you as enclosed a copy of an article
on the latest issue of Woman's Weekly captioned: "A Piece
of Advice to American Institute in Taiwan -- Please
Remember. We Are Not Refugees."

    The irony is that while all the major newspapers
and influential magazines have, thus far, restrained to
report and comment this unpleasant situation for fear of
aggravating the existing delicate relations between us,
a soft-purring Woman's Weekly, equivalent to your Ladies
Journal, should see fit to fire the first salvo at AIT.
I suggest you ask the Library of Congress to translate the
whole text and pass the English version to the State
Department for study and comments.

    Again, I want to thank you very sincerely for your
kind letter. I send my very best regards from both myself
and Cecillia to all of your lovely family.

Sincerely,

C. P. Chang
President

P.S. I was very pleased to learn from the Business Week of
July 16 that George Dalley is going to be appointed as
next Chairman of Civil Aviation Board.

中華民國台北市敦化南路610號 (林肯大廈4樓) 電話：7089640 · 7054331~9

C.P. Chang, President
Hwa Mei International Development, Inc.
4th Floor, 610 Tun Hwa S. Road
Taipei, Taiwan R.O.C.

Dear C.P.:

The State Department has just gotten back to
me regarding my inquiry on your behalf concerning
the visa problems in Taiwan. I've learned the
following:

There's definitely been a problem with the
volume of non-immigrant visas in Taipei. The long
delay in providing visas to businessmen and tour-
ists resulted from three factors. First, no visas
were issued from March 1 to April 23 because the
American Institute in Taiwan (AIT) was waiting
for reprogrammed funds which Congress refused to
approve. A backlog of over 10,000 applications
piled up during this period. Second, beginning in
January 1979 the authorities on Taiwan for the
first time began to issue tourist passports lead-
ing to a huge increase in the number of visitors
who applied for travel to the U.S. Third, visitor
visa applications normally peak in July and August
as over 3500 students from Taiwan prepare to enter
U.S. colleges and universities.

The State Department has been working closely
with AIT in attempting to solve this temporary
problem. AIT's staff in Taipei has hired additional temporary personnel, and regular staff members
are helping out in the visa lines. On July 17 AIT
received a report from Taipei stating that this
personnel augmentation, along with streamlined
administration procedures has succeeded in eliminating
the lines outside the visa office. It looks as though
the problem is now well in hand, and gradually the
time required for processing visa applications should
be reduced.

Again, it was great to hear from you. I feel
certain the crisis point in this situation has
passed, but by all means let me know if I can be
of further help.

With warmest regards,

Sincerely,

Richard Moe
Chief of Staff

October 4, 1979

Mr. C.P. Chang, President
Hwa Mei International Development, Inc.
4th Floor, 610 Tun Hwa South Rd.
Taipei, Taiwan ROC

Dear C.P.:

Thanks so much for your thoughtful letter. I understand your concern about the air agreement, but as I mentioned to you when you were in Washington, I would hope it would not have an adverse effect upon the relations between our two peoples. We're all anxious that it not, but I'm taking the liberty of sending your letter around so that the thoughtful points you make are not lost on anyone here.

Many thanks for your kindness in writing. It was great to see you while you were in town. I look forward to seeing you again soon.

With warmest regards,

Sincerely,

Richard Moe
Chief of Staff

104

United States Senate

WASHINGTON, D.C.

RICHARD (DICK) STONE
FLORIDA

September 11, 1979

Dear C.P.:

Thanks for your nice note and for
mentioning Cecillia's availability and
her offer of assistance which I very much
appreciate.

Please convey my congratulations to
Fred on his well-merited elevations. I am
still looking forward to bringing my family
out if at all possible during the Christmas
vacation.

Hope to see you soon.

With warm regards.

Most cordially,

Dick

1980s

台灣經濟開始起飛，逐漸步入經貿大國的地位，幾乎每種台灣產品外銷都創下世界第一的紀錄，並與南韓，香港及新加坡合稱亞洲四小龍。然此時期，台灣的邦交國僅剩三十個左右。但隨著台灣經濟改善，台灣旅遊人口與日增加，與台灣沒有邦交的國家，便以非官方辦事處的身份，在台灣「代為受理」申請簽證。從這個方面來講，台灣目前的外交成果，其實是因為民眾在經濟上的努力，換來了其他國家的尊重。

一九八〇年，仇家彪先生擔任中歐貿易促進會副秘書長。中歐貿易促進會為半官方民間組織，為促進台灣與歐洲國家經貿關係而成立。

THE WHITE HOUSE

WASHINGTON

May 20, 1983

Dear C.P.:

I enjoyed visiting with you over the telephone. I trust
your daughter's wedding went well. From what you tell me
about how well she did at Maryland in Computer Sciences, I
am sure she has a wonderful career ahead of her.

Thank you for alerting Mr. Lon, the Director General of the
Chinese Institute in Vienna, about my impending residence
there as the U.S. Ambassador to International Organizations,
including the International Atomic Energy Agency.   I
look forward to contact with him when I arrive in Vienna.

Hopefully, I can find reason to visit Taiwan, either in an
official or unofficial capacity, in the near future.

In the meantime, best wishes to you for continued success.
If your activities for the EuroAsia Trade Organization bring
you to Vienna, I certainly hope you will contact me. Both
Jane and I would love to host a dinner for you.

Kind personal regards.

                          Cordially,

                          Richard S. Williamson
                          Assistant to the President
                          for Intergovernmental Affairs

Mr. C.P. Chiang
EuroAsia Trade Organization
4F, No. 1 Hsu Chow Road
Taipai, Taiwan ROC

Dear C. P. and Celia,

1986 is almost history. Another year has quickly passed. Once again, we have much for which to be thankful.

Among the year's highlights was the wedding of our first-born, Mark, to Betty. We are delighted to have Betty as our new daughter-in-law. She is a lovely young Christian who, among other things, has served as a short-term missionary to Haiti. For their honeymoon last spring, they journeyed to Austria, Germany, Hungary and Romania. In Romania, they ministered to persecuted Christians. In March, they will make us grandparents once again. The enclosed picture gives you a glimpse of their lovely wedding in Massachusetts, where they continue to live.

Another highlight was the doctor's pronouncement in May that he didn't understand it, but Ann's blood white count was "nearly back to normal." The leukemia diagnosis of two years ago is not a current threat. For this, we sincerely and literally thank God. The doctor may not understand it, but we think we do. Our God is ALL powerful!

In June, Ann, Patty and I spent a great week in Hawaii. I conducted a campaign training seminar for a couple days and then we played in the sand and toured Oahu Island. What a delight!

Without a doubt, the worst event of the year was when Jim, Linda and our two precious grandsons moved to Quincy, IL, where Jim is the youth pastor of a Baptist Church. They are doing very well, but we sure miss them. We managed to visit them for a week in August and they spent Thanksgiving week with us, so we've seen them, but it sure is far less desirable than having them nearby every day. In May, they will present us with another grandchild, hopefully a girl.

Jeff is still in his own apartment nearby. He has taken up the hobby of remote-controlled airplanes. He's done a good job of building two airplanes and really enjoys finding the time (and money) to fly them. After four years of running the printing presses for the Congressional committee where I used to work, Jeff got laid off because of funding curtailments. He's now working in construction.

Patty is still working for Entre Computer headquarters and is doing very well. She recently had her first business trip to help with a trade show in Dallas. In January she will have her second business trip -- this time to Acapulco, Mexico. She continues to be a real delight as our last child at home. She's developing great skills in the kitchen, particularly in making fancy gingerbread houses and chocolate Easter baskets. In fact, she made pretty good money last Easter by making and selling Easter baskets at her office.

Ann and I did more travelling than usual this year, most of it business related. Trips included Phoenix, Portland, Los Angeles, Fort Collins (CO), Hilton Head (SC), and the fancy Greenbrier Resort in West Virginia.

At long last, we have architectural drawings under way for expanding our kitchen, dining room and porch. The improvements will add delightful features to the livability of our house. Ann will be the general contractor and you can be sure she will obtain quality work for a fair price. She has always been expert at that.

109

Most of my work this year has been in running the Free Congress Political Action Committee. Our primary role is to train and help elect conservatives to the Congress. Judging from the results of the Senate elections, it would seem we didn't have much success. We did far better in the House. In 1987, I will shift my focus slightly and concentrate on elections at the state level rather than the federal level.

We trust you had a good year and we hope to get an update on your latest happenings. May God grant you a blessed Christmas and a very special 1987.

With much love,

Dick

Dick and Ann Dingman

Thanks for the lovely appointment Diary. I will put it to good use.

1990s

中華民國政府開始嘗試以聯合國能接受的名義，尋求重返聯合國及其他國際組織。一九九〇年一月，台灣以「台澎金馬關稅領域」名義，申請加入關稅與貿易總協定（GATT）。而台灣更在一九九一年，以「中華台北」（Chinese Taipei）的名義，和中國、香港同時加入亞太經合會（APEC）。更重要的是，一九九三年，更提出了重返聯合國的主張。自此以後，台灣參與聯合國的議題，再度成為台灣外交活動當中，相當重要的工作目標。

一九九〇年，仇家彪先生擔任中歐貿易促進會秘書長。

一九九三至一九九六年，仇家彪先生擔任中歐貿易促進會顧問。

P. O. Box 168
Mount Vernon
VA 22121
October 29, 1991

C.P. Chang
Secretary General
Euro-Asia Trade Organization
4th Floor
1 Hsu Chow Road
Taipei, Taiwan
Republic of China

Dear C. P.:

Using the Appointment Diary you sent me reminded me of you recently and our many long talks in the past about developments in the R.O.C. This train of thought led me to send you the enclosed memorandum I have written on a hot, current subject and to see what your recollection is regarding the issue.

As you will see from the memo, which I prepared only for reasons of analysis, the subject·matter is the action of the DPP to call for replacement of the R.O.C. with a new nation-state known as the Republic of Taiwan. What particularly concerned me is the fact that the DPP is cloaking its proposal under the claimed protection of the Taiwan Relations Act.

One thing that Senator Goldwater and I carefully watched during Congressional debate on the TRA was any effort, especially by Senator Pell, to slip in language on the subject of changing the form of government. Senator Goldwater remained on the Floor or in the side chamber ready to object to any such amendment. Similarly, I tried to keep guard against anything referring to a break-away nation.

After reviewing the law, I believe my first impression is right: the TRA does not address, nor apply, to the situation of a separate Taiwan nation, that is, an entirely new international state. This fact means that the DPP's proposal would leave the people in the Taiwan region without any diplomatic or legislative recognition under U.S. law.

This issue involves political as well as legal aspects, both of which I seek to cover in the brief memo. I would be interested in knowing what your private reaction is to this controversy. And, Margrit joins me in wishing you the best of health and continued success. Our greetings also go to Cecilia.

Sincerely,

J. Terry Emerson

112

13923 Brandy Oaks Place
Chesterfield
Virginia 23832-2720
December 31, 1992

Mr. C. P. Chang
Deputy Secretary General
Euro-Asia Trade Organization
4th Floor, 1 Hsu Chow Road
Taipei, Taiwan
Republic of China

Dear C. P.:

Thank you once again for the outstanding desk diary and calendar.
It is always my main appointment book for the year ahead.

What a year the ROC had in 1992. Approval at last of F-16 fighter
jet sales. A visit from Carla Hills, the first cabinet-level U.S.
official to appear publicly since 1979.

Further steps on the way to a peaceful unification of China.
Booming indirect trade between the ROC and the Mainland, with Taiwan
investments reaching as far as Sinkiang. The ROC application for
GATT membership finally put on the working agenda of the GATT ruling
council.

The massive infrastructure transformation of Taiwan under the
ROC's 775 project Six Year Development Plan, the envy of Clinton
economists. And, not least, the bold and risky fast steps towards
Constitutional reform and full democratization.

So much is happening so fast in the ROC, it is difficult to stand
back and look at it all together. Each component of change and
modernization is important in its own right, and success with any single
plan would be accomplishment enough for most countries of the world.
But the cumulative impact of the wide range of reforms being put into
place by the ROC will virtually make a new nation, one capable of
a role of leadership in nurturing peace, healthy world trade with
global economic growth, and stable, democratic societies.

The challenges are enormous, but I have every confidence the
will and genius of the free Chinese people will succeed. Best wishes,
my friend, for a truly good New Year.

Margrit and I would much enjoy seeing and talking with you again,
so please let us know whenever you might be visiting the Washington,
D.C. area. Although we have just recently moved South to a suburb of
Richmond, we return to Washington at least every two weeks and would
definitely make the trip in order to visit with you again.

Sincerely,

J. Terry Emerson

113

中歐貿易促進會

C. P. CHANG
SECRETARY GENERAL
EURO-ASIA TRADE ORGANIZATION

January 20, 1993

Mr. J. Terry Emerson
13923 Brandy Oaks Place
Chesterfield
Virginia 23832-2720
U. S. A.

Dear Terry:

I am extremely delighted to receive your letter of Dec. 31, 1992, and I am equally happy to share with your views on the remarkable achievements the ROC has made in 1992, even though most of us are still not used to the jostling and fist fighting on the floors of both our Legislative Yuan and National Assembly.

Looking back, I must say that friends like Senator Goldwater and Terry Emerson have been instrumental in helping turn, or coach, the ROC from a struggling economy and a fledgling democracy into a prosperous and full fledged democratic nation in the rising Asia Pacific Region over the past two decades. Indeed, we have come a long way, but I will never forget the genuine friendship and staunch support that I had always received from you during my four year tour of duty with our Embassy in Washington, D.C. Even after 16 years, I could still see vividly in my memory the lone figure of Terry Emerson distributing his paper in defending the ROC constitution and its political system during the first hearing on Taiwan's human rights held by the House Foreign Affairs Committee in 1977.

I am very glad to note your encouraging tone in your letter on the prospect of a peaceful unification of China. I deeply believe this is not only important to the Chinese people everywhere, but also vital to the stability of a world that is going through great turmoils in the post cold war era. To meet this new challenge, I have decided to retire from my present position as Secretary General of Euro-Asia Trade Organization at the end of March and to spend more time in doing volunteer work on the Mainland in the future.

.../2

3RD FL., 9 ROOSEVELT RD., SEC. 2 TAIPEI. TAIWAN. REPUBLIC OF CHINA FAX:886-2-3928393 TEL:3932115

中歐貿易促進會

C. P. CHANG
SECRETARY GENERAL
EURO-ASIA TRADE ORGANIZATION

- 2 -

In fact, I had a test run in May and September last year in accepting invitations to give speeches and lectures on "Single European Market" and "European Economic and Political Integration" in Shanghai and Peking. The response was overwhelming, and I was convinced that my expertise on European integration could be a conduit in contributing, in a small way, to making the mainland Chinese trade officials and academicians realize that in the face of economic globalization and trade regionalization, they really have no choice but seek Taiwan's trade and investment without, first, getting a political settlement on their terms.

You may say it's a sort of Peace Corps mission -- C.P. style. Therefore, in planning my early retirement, I am quite relieved, almost happy actually; because it gives me a feeling of inner freedom and self-confirmation. It is one of the paradoxes of my life that I am experiencing such a creative feeling at the thought of my retirement.

Knowing your interest in the economic development of the ROC and its future role in the world economy, I am enclosing my speeches in Reykjavik and Paris for your reference so that you may share with me some of my thoughts on our past performance and the challenges we are facing in the 90s.

Cecilia joins me in sending you and Margrit our warmest regards and best wishes for a prosperous year of 1993.

Sincerely,

C. P. Chang

C. P. Chang

3RD FL., 9 ROOSEVELT RD., SEC. 2 TAIPEI. TAIWAN. REPUBLIC OF CHINA FAX:886-2-3928393 TEL:3932115

115

13923 Brandy Oaks Pl.
Chesterfield
VA 23832-2720
U.S.A.
February 05, 1993

The Honorable C. P. Chang
Secretary General
Euro-Asia Trade Organizatior
Taipei, Taiwan
R.O.C.

Dear C. P.:

Margrit and I just returned from a return visit to Arizona
where Senator Goldwater was the center of attention once again as
the recipient of an extremely generous award from the Republic of
China to the Goldwater Chair of American Institution at Arizona
State University. We are leaving for Switzerland in two days for
another nostalgic return to Margrit's native country.

Upon arriving home, I discovered your letter of January 20
and the two outstanding speeches delivered by you in Europe recently.
C. P., the quality of these speeches is truly excellent.

First, they are honest. Your integrity shows through the
statements in the remarks. Second, they are very well written
and organized. Third, they are interesting.

There are only minor points of difference in emphasis that we
may have. For example, I, too, recognize that Communist China has
made strenuous efforts to promote foreign trade. However, I would
then follow up by pointing out that it has been at the expense of the
United States. Red China's trade surplus with America is about
$18 billion this year. The R.O.C. surplus has fallen, in contrast,
to about $7 or $8 billion. The R.O.C. buys twice as much from
us as the mainland, which is amazing considering the size of your
nation. (Also, Red China is the only major power who is still
increasing its military spending, a fact that disturbs me a great
deal.)

C. P., I am impressed most of all by your vision, and by your
unending dedication to the ultimate goal of a united, free and
stable China. Margrit and I know that you will be productive,
happy and successful in what you may call a retirement, but what
I know will call upon all your energies and experience in the
important future ahead.

Sincerely,

J. Terry Emerson

P.S. I hope to get a briefing on the ROC's GATT application in
Zurich this month, a matter you must be following closely.

DANTE B. FASCELL
19TH DISTRICT, FLORIDA

FOREIGN AFFAIRS COMMITTEE
CHAIRMAN

ARMS CONTROL, INTERNATIONAL
SECURITY AND SCIENCE SUBCOMMITTEE
CHAIRMAN

SELECT COMMITTEE ON NARCOTICS
ABUSE AND CONTROL
MEMBER

Congress of the United States
House of Representatives
Washington, DC 20515-0919

CHARLES R. O'REGAN
ADMINISTRATIVE ASSISTANT

COMMISSION ON SECURITY AND
COOPERATION IN EUROPE
MEMBER

NORTH ATLANTIC ASSEMBLY
CHAIRMAN
HOUSE DELEGATION

CANADA—UNITED STATES
INTERPARLIAMENTARY GROUP
MEMBER, U.S. DELEGATION

December 8, 1992

Mr. C.P. Chang
Deputy Secretary General for Administration
Euro-Asia Trade Organization
4th Floor, 1 Hsu Chow Road
Taipei, Taiwan
Republic of China

Dear C.P.:

Many thanks for the beautiful 1993 appointment diary. You are very kind to remember me after all these years.

As you know, Chairman Fascell is retiring at the end of the year and so shall I -- at least from Capitol Hill. Following your lead, I hope to pursue a second career, either in the private sector or in the new Clinton adminis-tration. I trust that, wherever I am located, our paths will continue to cross.

I may be reached at 1514 North Buchanan Street, Arlington, Virginia, 22205, telephone 703-527-1629, after the first of the year. If you ever get to Washington, I hope you will contact me.

My best to you and Cecelia in the new year.

Cordially,

CHARLES R. O'REGAN
Administrative Assistant

COR/o

117

中歐貿易促進會

C. P. CHANG
SECRETARY GENERAL
EURO-ASIA TRADE ORGANIZATION

January 13, 1993

Mr. Charles R. O'Regan
1514 North Buchanan Street
Arlington, VA 22205
U. S. A.

Dear Bob:

It was with mixed emotions that I received your announcement about your retirement from Capitol Hill. I sincerely hope you will enjoy great success in your new ventures either in the private sector or in the new Clinton administration.

However, I must confess disappointment over the fact that a good and true friend of the Republic of China on Taiwan has left the U.S. Congress. I am also a little sad to see the Capitol Hill lose such an able and dedicated foreign affairs expert at a time when the United States is at the cross roads in finding its new role in the rapidly changing world.

As you leave the U.S. Congress, do so knowing in your heart that I value your friendship, respect your integrity, admire you for your dedication and ability and wish you for your good health, much happiness and all the best in life.

I am grateful that Bob O'Regan happened to cross my path during my tour of duty in our Embassy in Washington, D.C. And, again, my deepest appreciation for all your many kindnesses, and the hope that you will continue to stay in touch with me.

With my warmest regards and best wishes,

Sincerely,

C. P. Chang

C. P. Chang

3RD FL., 9 ROOSEVELT RD., SEC. 2 TAIPEI. TAIWAN. REPUBLIC OF CHINA FAX:886-2-3928393 TEL:3932115

118

中歐貿易促進會

C. P. CHANG
SECRETARY GENERAL
EURO-ASIA TRADE ORGANIZATION

January 18, 1993

Mr. Roy A. Werner
28 Foxhill
Irvine, CA 92714-3066
U. S. A.

Dear Roy:

It is so nice to hear from you and to learn that you are planning to rejoin the government at a time when the United States is at the cross roads in finding its new role in the rapidly changing world. I wish you every success in securing a more challenging position in the new Clinton administration.

As to my own plan for the year of 1993, I have decided to retire from my present position as Secretary General of Euro-Asia Trade Organization (EATO) at the end of March. As you know, I had spent the full decade of 80s in promoting Taiwan to European countries and now I should consider my work completed. So I can now add the 13 year endeavor with the EATO to my 17 year career in the navy and 11 year in the civil service and foreign service. Is it possible that could all add up to 41 years?

But I'll not be loafing away my time in Taipei. On the contrary, I'll be starting a new life or rather a kind of "born again" life. In fact I had a test run in May and September last year in accepting invitations to give speeches and lectures on "Single European Market" and "European Economic and Political Integration" in Shanghai and Peking on the Mainland. The response was overwhelming, and I was convinced that my expertise on European integration could be a conduit in contributing, in a small way, to making the mainland Chinese trade officials and academicians realize that in the face of economic globalization and trade regionalization, they really have no choice but seek Taiwan's trade and investment without, first, getting a political settlement on their terms.

.../2

中歐貿易促進會

C. P. CHANG
SECRETARY GENERAL
EURO-ASIA TRADE ORGANIZATION

So, I'll continue my volunteer work and spend more time in the Mainland to spread my "gospel" this year and next. You may say it's a sort of Peace Corps mission -- C.P. style. Therefore, in planning my early retirement, I am quite relieved, almost happy actually; because it gives me a feeling of inner freedom and self-confirmation. It is one of the paradoxes of my life that I am experiencing such a creative feeling at the thought of my retirement.

Good luck, my dear friend, for your great success in the "born again" Democratic administration. But wherever you will be working for the U.S. government, please give us a helping hand and moral support. I know you'll be too glad to do this, because you have always been one of the staunchest friends and supporters of the Republic of China on Taiwan.

I am grateful that Roy Werner and his family, and his friends, happened to cross my path 19 years ago. I hope you will continue to stay in touch with me; and I want you to know that our prayers go with you and your family.

Sincerely,

C. P. Chang

3RD FL., 9 ROOSEVELT RD., SEC. 2 TAIPEI.TAIWAN. REPUBLIC OF CHINA FAX:886-2-3928393 TEL:3932115

中歐貿易促進會

C. P. CHANG
SECRETARY GENERAL
EURO-ASIA TRADE ORGANIZATION

January 20, 1993

Mr. David A. Rust
114 Calbert Road
Rockville, Md. 20850-3812
U. S. A.

Dear Dave,

Upon return to Taipei from an overseas trip, I hasten to write you to say how sorry I am to miss the opportunity of meeting your friend Miss Kelly Hughes during her visit to Taipei. On the other hand, I am very pleased to learn that you have moved to the Department of Agriculture to take up a more challenging position. I wish you all the best and great success in your new appointment.

As to my own plan for the year of 1993, I have decided to retire from my present position as Secretary General of Euro-Asia Trade Organization (EATO) at the end of March. Putting together my years in the navy, civil service and foreign service with my 13 years with the EATO, it all adds up to 41 years. Is it possible that I have been working for 41 years ?

But I'll not be loafing away my time in Taipei. On the contrary, I'll be starting a new life or rather a kind of "born again" life. In fact, you might be surprised to hear that I had a test run in May and September last year in accepting invitations to give speeches and lectures on "Single European Market" and "European Economic and Political Integration" in Shanghai and Peking on mainland China. The response was overwhelming, and I was convinced that my expertise on European integration could be a conduit in contributing, in a small way, to making the mainland Chinese trade officials and academicians realize that in the face of economic globalization and trade regionalization, they really have no choice but seek Taiwan's trade and investment without, first, getting a political settlement on their terms.

.../2

中歐貿易促進會

C. P. CHANG
SECRETARY GENERAL
EURO-ASIA TRADE ORGANIZATION

So, I'll continue my volunteer work and spend more time in Mainland to spread my "gospel" this year and next. You may say it's a sort of Peace Corps mission -- C.P. style. Therefore, in planning my early retirement, I am quite relieved, almost happy actually; because it gives me a feeling of inner freedom and self-confirmation. It is one of the paradoxes of my life that I am experiencing such a creative feeling at the thought of my retirement.

I am grateful that Dave Rust and his family, and his friends, happened to cross my path 19 years ago. I hope you will continue to stay in touch with me, and I want you to know that our prayers go with you and your family.

Sincerely,

C. P. Chang

P.S. Cecilia sends her warmest regards to you and Pam.

3RD FL., 9 ROOSEVELT RD., SEC. 2 TAIPEI. TAIWAN. REPUBLIC OF CHINA FAX:886-2-3928393 TEL:3932115

1280 - 21st St., N.W. # 607
Washington, D. C. 20036

February 28, 1994

Dear C. P.:

My last letter to you addressed to
Euro-Asia was hopefully received but since
I had no reply from you I am not sure!
In early November, I received an appointment
from President Clinton to the Department of
Defense and was assigned to handle liaison
for the Secretary of Defense with the
retired military community and veterans
organizations. Since that time, of course,
Aspin resigned, Admiral Inman was nominated,
withdrew and just within the last few weeks
we are trying to get organized with the new
Secetary, William Perry. Only with Speaker
Foley's persistence did the appointment happen
because the Clinton crowd tend sto be young
and distrusting of anyone over 50.:= In any
case, I will play this out for a year and then
return to Texas.

You are obviously now involved in your
new endeavor and I am so anxious to have an
update. You see, so many of your friends in
Washington expect me to keep them up to date
on your endeavors and I cannot do that unless
you tell me. Ha. Seriously, you have many
wonderful friends in Washington (including me)
and they are all thinking the best for you
and Cecelia. You left your mark here and
can be very proud for establishing lifetime
friendships. When I read the enclosed article
in the Post, I thought "yes, that's the
classy way my friends in Taiwan do things.
Hope this reaches you. I expect to be in
San Diego later in March and will try to contact
your daughter and son in law. Please write.

Sincerely your friend,

123

中 歐 貿 易 促 進 會
EURO-ASIA TRADE ORGANIZATION

March 18, 1994

Mr. C. Dayle Henington
1280 21st St., N.W. # 607
Washington, D.C. 20036
U. S. A.

Dear Dayle:

I was very happy to receive your letter of Feb. 28, 1994, giving me a run down about your odyssey in the Clinton Administration. I can fully understand your feeling about having to work and deal with those young turks who believe they are going to save America.

This was exactly what happened to me that inspired my thought of an early retirement so that I could avoid having to associate with the rising generation of arrogant and taking-everything-for-granted young bureaucrats. Therefore, when I finally retired as secretary general of Euro-Asia Trade Organization (EATO) at the end of March last year, I was quite relieved, almost happy actually, because always when I accomplished something or made an important decision, it gave me a feeling of inner freedom and self-confirmation. Indeed, it is one of the paradoxes of my life that I was experiencing such a creative feeling at the thought of my retirement.

Although I am now retired from executive work, I still serve as advisor at EATO. If I am not travelling, I go to my office everyday to do research on European integration in particular and the world economy in general. Besides, I have been giving lectures and speeches both in Taiwan and in mainland China. I was even invited by Business Week to attend, as a panelist, the "1993 BusinessWeek Asia Symposium of Chief Executives" in Shanghai in September 1993. Enclosed in the letter is a copy of my speech which you might find interesting.

Since retirement, I have been very active in doing volunteer lecture work on the mainland, because I am convinced that Taiwan can share its political and economic reform experiences with the mainland. To the mainland Chinese, Taiwan's experience can be a source of inspiration and aspiration. On the other hand, I sincerely believe that only Chinese on Taiwan can help change their ideology and way of thinking, thus making them more enlightened and civilized, and less a menace to the world. In April and May last year, I made a lecture tour of 38 days in seven major commercial centers including Shanghai and Peking, and gave 13 speeches and attended five discussion meetings for students and faculty in universities and for trade officials and managers of businesses on the following subjects: (1) Taiwan's experience in economic development, (2) A review on the development of world trade and the prospect of the world's regionalization on trade and economy, and (3) The impacts of NAFTA and Single European Market on the economy of Asian countries.

3RD FL., 9 ROOSEVELT RD., SEC. 2 TAIPEI. TAIWAN. REPUBLIC OF CHINA FAX:886-2-3928393 TEL:3932115

In late April, I'll travel again to the mainland for a 3-week lecture tour, extending from coastal cities to the inland Sichuan Province in the South West. The highlight will be my two lectures to a group of 150 Shanghai chief executives of big industries organized by the Shanghai Municipal government.

You might be interested to know that I am now highly respected and well-liked by many communist Chinese officials who greatly appreciate my good intention to educate their people in the field of international trade. That is certainly a far cry from my work in Washington, D.C. in the seventies. Talking about 70s now, I have suddenly realized that we first met in Taipei in January 1974 when you visited the ROC with a congressional delegation. Imagine that was over 20 years ago! We were much younger then and we had a lot of fun together. The great thing is that we have been great pals since and have kept in touch. But the happy thing I feel for you is that you now have Juli to keep your company. She is a great girl and I adore her. Otherwise, I would definitely feel bad whenever I think of my pal Dayle Henington living alone miserably in Texas. Isn't San Antonio a desert place or a fortress surrounded by Mexican Amigos? Ha Ha!

Michele and our grand daughter were visiting us during the Chinese New Year in February. Alas, she is now more than 50% American and her daughter 100%. She told me that you will visit San Diego and she is looking forward to seeing you again after so many years. If I am correct, the last time you saw her was in May 1983 at her wedding. Time certainly flies and I am getting hopelessly nostalgic.

So, that's all I can tell you at the moment. I hope I have kept you up-to-date on my life in Taiwan. Please say hello to my old friends on the Capital Hill and tell them I missed them and Washington, D.C. But more important, tell them that I had learned from them a great deal, not only in American politics, but also about American decency which is really what makes America a great nation and Americans a great people. I love you all with my whole heart.

Cecilia joins me in sending you and Juli our warmest regards and best wishes.

Sincerely yours,

C. P. Chang

3RD FL., 9 ROOSEVELT RD., SEC. 2 TAIPEI. TAIWAN. REPUBLIC OF CHINA FAX:886-2-3928393 TEL:3932115

World Economy, China, and Asian Competitiveness

C. P. Chang's Opening Remarks

Presented at

The 1993 BusinessWeek Asia Symposium of Chief Executives

Shanghai, September 20-22, 1993

Mr. Chairman, Distinguished Guests, Ladies and Gentlemen:

It is a great privilege for me to have this opportunity to share views, Asian views, with such a distinguished gathering of world leaders in business. I especially appreciate the invitation from the Business Week who selects me to be one of the panelists for this forum.

Today, no nation is unaffected by the great changes taking place in the world. For example, the global economy has been both buffeted and presented with new opportunities by the sudden demise of communism in the former Soviet Union and East Europe, and by the rapid rise of prosperity in the Pacific Rim. These changes and more have created the need for major adjustment in the global economy.

But the most important event to affect world trade in 1993 is regionalization. The Single European Market is not alone. The establishment of ASEAN Free Trade Area is another recent example, while the North America Free Trade Area will be inaugurated on Jan. 1, 1994, if everything goes well. Furthermore, the increasing activities of Asia-Pacific Economic Community, or APEC, is picking up steam on the horizon of regional trade picture.

Especially noteworthy is the rise of prosperity and economic power in East Asia. Asia's four Little Dragons -- Taiwan, Hong Kong, Singapore and South Korea -- are following in the footsteps of Japan. Hot on their heels are mainland China, Malaysia and Thailand, and the other ASEAN powers.

The exciting emergence of the free economies of East Asia has created much talk about the coming of a "Pacific Century." At present, Asia already accounts for more than 23 per cent of world trade. In recent years, the traditional engines of world trade are slowing down. But most of Asia's export driven economies are growing at a rapid pace.

For the first time, Asian countries are confronted with simultaneous recessions in the world's three biggest markets, the United States, Europe and Japan. Yet, according to Asian Wall Street Journal's annual economy survey published in October 1992, "Many of the 12 Asian countries covered in the survey have managed to post respectable export gains, feeding off the region's own increasing prosperity. Asia is now its own largest customer, with intra-regional commerce accounting for more than 40 per cent of its

Page 2

total trade, up from about 30 per cent in 1986. This reflects a widening pool of middle class consumers outside Japan, increasingly growing intra-Asian investment and the rapid liberalization of some of the region's biggest economies, particularly mainland China."

Obviously, an increasingly important factor in the regional trade equation is mainland China, where continuing reform and rapid economic growth have attracted Asian investors, sparking double-digit growth and created a burgeoning market for everything from refrigerators to electric power plants.

However, headlong economic transformation is producing all kinds of problems and contradictions. Many of the problems mainland China faces in its rush to development are high inflation, corruption, speculation, disrespect for the law. This is a price mainland China is now paying for economic and social liberation. But history has shown us that when the economy grows too fast, crime will often grow with it. Mainland China is not alone in the world on that score. Based on my own observation throughout my 38-day lecture tour in seven major commercial centers in mainland China in April and May this year, I am convinced that mainland China can withstand the upheaval, created by the astonishing speed in its march toward the free market. I am hoping that mainland China will move faster to improve its legal system and enforce law and order more effectively so as to overcome modernization's worst excesses in the near future.

Looking ahead, we see the emergence of a Greater China that has the optimum combination of assets from all three Chinese-based economies -- the technological and manufacturing capability of Taiwan, the marketing and service strength of Hong Kong, and the abundant land and labor of mainland China. Within this Chinese-based economy system, unlike the European Community and the North America Free Trade Area which are established by treaties and agreements, the private sectors move rapidly over political boundaries, resulting in a "borderless economy," which is not motivated or supported by political force or government policy. The private sector of Greater China has been the force propelling regional economic integration and fueling the economic explosion, first in southern China and coastal provinces and, now, spreading to central and northern China.

When we study the contrast between Russia and East Europe and mainland China in their distinctly different outcome of economic reform, we must view it from a cultural perspective. While ethnic Russians and East Europeans have taken roots and settled comfortably in their adoptive countries, ethnic Chinese entrepreneurs abroad are busily creating a web of business contacts with mainland China. Along with businessmen in Taiwan and Hong Kong, the Chinese émigrés, who created the merchant class of Southeast Asia, are rushing to establish their footholds in mainland China through trade, investment and joint venture in recent years as a result of mainland China's economic and trade liberalization. This has, no doubt, helped open the floodgates for the release of the natural talents and entrepreneurial spirit of Chinese people. They now have the opportunity and the method to realize their true potential. These talents and spirit exist together in the Greater China, forming the primary fuel for its continued development as well as making it one of the foremost economic power houses of the century.

In just one generation, Taiwan went from an impoverished backwater to become a roaring little dragon. And in just a decade, mainland China has abandoned its Stalinist model of planned economy and adopted a market economy. Through a sweeping economic reform and trade liberalization a year ago, the economy is moving at a breakneck speed with 12.8% growth in 1992 and a sizzling 50% in the private sector. It must be unprecedented in history for an economy of mainland China's size, and it is now very difficult to turn off the engine of change when it involves as many places as it does in mainland China.

Ironically, industrialized countries are now fearing the continued fast growth of Greater China and worrying about its ability to export good-quality and less-expensive products to their markets, hence threatening their home industries, some of which have become senile and uncompetitive. On the contrary, I want to assure you that the fast growing Chinese-based economies are also thirsty for sophisticated equipment and machinery for building their infrastructures and expanding their industries, thereby creating a vast market for imports of high technology and capital equipment as well as consumer products from industrialized countries. I am more than convinced that the combined resources and efforts of Greater China in developing their economies are actually helping expand the world trade and investment and, thus, contributing, in large measures, to the revival of world economy. On the other hand, as a locomotive for the fast growth of other Asian economies, Greater China is even helping make East Asia less a westward-looking exporter and more a harmonized civilization that can stand and thrive on its own.

Looking to the future, I sincerely believe that the range of interaction among Taiwan, Hong Kong and mainland China will expand continuously and progressively. The road to definitive and substantive changes for tomorrow's China is now being paved. In the end, we may see that economic interests have superseded political ones and, in doing so, have pulled China into the 21st century.

It seems that I sound quite optimistic. But I am only trying to convey to you, my friends, a Taiwan Chinese view of how the world should adjust to the rise of a new China in the most positive manner.

Thank you for your attention.

Page 6

131

1280 - 21st St., N.W., # 607
Washington, D. C. 20036

June 16, 1994

Honorable C. P. Chang
Euro--Asia Trade Organization
3rd Fl., No. 9 Roosevelt Rd., Sec. 2
Taipei, Taiwan, Republic of China

Dear C. P.:

How rapidly the time passes when it becomes your own.
That is, once you've achieved the freedom to prepare your
time as you wish, it just isn't enough! Your letter of
March 18th was so informative that I sent copies to several
of your Washington friends and then we had a lunch to talk
about our impressive colleague in Taipei. Marshall Lynam
in particular has you as one of his heroes, as do I.

Your work sounds so interesting. What I would give
to make one of those trips to the mainland with you to
hear one of your presentations. Who knows, perhaps that
might be possible one day. Juli and I will conclude our
time in Washington at the end of October. We will re-
locate to San Antonio, Texas where Juli is likely to continue her employment with the home office of a company that
she works with here in government relations. We will look
forward to having you and Cecilia come and visit us once
we are settled in there. In addition, we plan to do some
travelling and want to come your way. Juli's daughter is a
flight attendant with United Airlines so we can get some
free passes and low price tickets. We will keep you supplied
with our address and phone, etc but until October, we will
be here at this address in Washington.

Michele and I did not manage a visit because my schedule
was so crazy. She did send me a photo of all of you taken
during her visit. She is a beautiful young lady (looks like
her mother). The daughter, also beautiful, looks like her
mother but in everyone is the C.P. eyes....alert, friendly,
compassionate and wise. We have the photo displayed with our
other special friends.

I do look forward to visiting with you, my friend, and
that is going to happen late this year or early next.
Keep in touch. Juli joins me in sending love and best
wishes.

Your friend,

C. Dayle Henington

132

Marshall L. Lynam
Government Relations Consultant
412 First St. S.E., Suite 60, Washington, D.C. 20003
202 544-7996

Mr. C.P. Chang   October 27, 1994
Euro-Asia Trade Organization
Third Floor, Number 9
Roosevelt Road, Section 2
Taipei, Taiwan
Republic of China

Dear C.P.:

In *She Stoops to Conquer*, written in 1773, Goldsmith said: "I love everything that's old--old friends, old times, old manners, old books, old wine...and old friends are best!"

Old friend, how have you been? It's been many years since we have had a chance to see each other. I talk often with Dayle Henington and Sherry Boehlert, and we reminisce about the great old days of which you were so much a part. I hope the years have treated you and Cecilia kindly, and you are enjoying the rewards of your good work.

With this letter to you I am sending a copy of a two-page letter I wrote to Fred Chien. I know you and Fred were very close, and I would like to ask that you, too, talk with my friends who will be in Taipei at the Grand Hyatt on December 12.

My friends, as the other letter explains, are Jeff Fegan and Terry Parent. They are hoping to interest China Airlines and EVA in direct passenger service to Dallas/Fort Worth International Airport.

I don't know anybody who is more qualified than you and Fred Chien to give wise counsel to Jeff and Terry. When you receive these letters, give the matter some thought and then please call me--collect, of course--at 202 544-7996. I'd like to hear whatever thoughts you have on how to make their visit most effective. Also, if Fred agrees to see Jeff and Terry, would it be appropriate for you to accompany them? I know that you and Fred were very close, and I presume you have remained so through the years.

Thank you, old friend. Eddie joins me in sending all the best to you and Cecilia and all your family.

Sincerely,

Marshall

Marshall L. Lynam

133

Father's Day - 1994

Dear C.P.:

Since I have not qualified for
"grandfather" status as yet, I must depend
on my good friend, C. P., to explain all
the joys of it. Actually, if one looks
at your photo on this cup, no explanation
is required because it says it all!

The photo is priceless and is now
displayed on the top of our piano, along
with other photos of our very special
friends. I couldn't resist having the
photo placed on this cup so each morning
when you enjoy your coffee, you can glance
at your special treasures of this life.

Juli and I will re-locate to San
Antonio, Texas in October, 1994 and then
be in touch with you about coordinating
Juli's first visit to Taiwan in early '95.

Our love to you and Cecilia.

Your friend,
Dayle

June 30, 1994

Dear Michele:

I am sending along a Father's Day gift for C.P. and there is a note to him tucked inside the cup. Perhaps you will be good enough to enclose it in one of your periodic shipments or hold it until you see them again.

Juli and I will be moving to Texas at the end of September but will be in touch from there, giving you addresses, etc. because we expect to have the time then to travel to delightful places like San Diego where we can see you.

Hope you and Jim are fine. Our best wishes always.

Sincerely,

C. Dayle Henington

10955 Wurzbach Rd., # 104
San Antonio, Texas 78230

January 7, 1995

Dear C.P.:

Today, the Euro-Asia Trade Organization calendar
arrived. You have been kind in sending me this
calendar over the years and I enjoy having it on my
desk to remind me of a very special friendship. I
am glad you received the coffee cup and no problem
that you didn't thank me until now!

At the end of September, we closed up shop in
Washington, took a two week trip to Italy and then returned to our new home in San Antonio. Juli is working
for the same company she was with in Washington.
Presently, I am enjoying my freedom after so many years
but may explore a couple of projects with some of my
friends in Mexico but I am in no hurry. We do want to
find a good time to visit Taiwan because I know how
wonderful it would be to show Juli your part of the
world and have some good times with you and Cecilia.
We definitely will coordinate with you before planning
the trip because you would be the main reason for coming.
I would like to do a side trip to Hong Kong since Juli
has never been there but we would want to spend the
majority of our time in Taiwan.

About six hours driving time from San Antonio, to
the west, is Big Bend National Park. My oldest son,
Greg (age 38) operatives a river company there on the
Rio Grande River. He takes people down the river for
from 1 to 3 days and nights. The mountains are awesome
and the city folks get a real charge out of these trips.
When you come to San Antonio, I want to take you. Why
can't you and Cecilia come here from San Diego the next
time you come to the States and spend a few days with us.
We have plenty of room and I could make you a Texan
pretty quick! By the way, Marshall Lynam brought a group
to go down the river in November and we had a great time.

136

You work in China sounds fascinating. You are offering
them invaluable guidance that will pay off I am sure.
This week, the enclosed story was in our San Antonio
paper. Do you know the Sino Aerospace Investment Corp.
in Taiwan? From my visits with Michelle by letter it
sounds like they are real Californians now. I thought
it was your plan to spend more time in California.

My friends in Washington are still trying to get over the
election and accept what happened. Speaker Foley was
defeated as you know and then was offered our Embassy in
China but I was not surprised that he didn't accept that.
He would like the London Embassy but a former Chairman
of our Joint Staff, Admiral Crowe has that for the moment.
And I can't believe Clinton will have another term.
I will not be able to vote for him myself because I
witnessed first hand his inability to get things together
in Washington.

President Bush's son was elected Governor of Texas. He
had another son, Jeb, who ran for Governor of Florida but
didn't make it. The former President lives in Houston
and is enjoying himself I'm told.

Well, thanks again for your Christmas note. All the best
to you and your family for 1995. Juli sends her love.

Sincerely,

P.S.

Our phone number is Area Code 210/558-8639.

10955 Wurzbach Road, # 104
San Antonio, Texas 78230

May 23, 1995

Dear C. P.,

There are not too many days that I do not think
about you, my friend, because Taiwan can be found on
almost any page of our media from day to day. The
enclosed clipping especially reminds me of the
never likely to be equalled efforts of your government,
under Fred, S. K. and C.P.'s leadership, to establish
in the American Congress deep and abiding respect for
your country's friendship and accomplishments. You
certainly can be proud of having played a key part in
an effort that continues to bring benefits to your
country and will for a long time to come.

I would like nothing better than to have a visit
with you and Cecelia. Had hoped that a trip to your
part of the world would have been possible before now
and it would have if I had come alone, but I would
very much like to include Juli in the next trip because
she has never been. When we moved to San Antonio in
October of last year, she elected to continue with the
insurance group she was working for in Washington and
whose home office is here in San Antonio. Primarily
this is due to the fact that in the late summer of '96
she will be fully vested (meaning rights to retirement
benefits) in the company and felt it was the right thing
to do to add another notch of financial security.
She has a challenging job and enjoys it but we are both
looking forward to being able to travel together without
any obstacles.

One thing that has occurred to me is that you
should let me know when you plan a visit to San Diego
because I would be more than glad to hop out there just
to have dinner with you one evening.

We enjoy San Antonio and do not miss the crazy pace
we kept up for so many years in Washington. And too,
the place is not the same as when you and I were there.
There is less respect and less ability in my view.
There are no Congressman Poages left as far as I can see.

Juli and I send special love and friendship to you
and your family. When you have a few minutes, please
give me a letter to welcome heartily.

138

June 21, 1995

Dear C. P.,

Since I wrote you a rather lengthy
letter recently, I will make this one
short. I thought this article in the
Washington Post was one you would enjoy
reading.

With regard to your President's
recent trip to the U. S. to receive his
honorary degree, I thought the manner in
which your government handled the entire
matter was just superb. Of course, the
vote in the Congress continues to reflect
the incredible job you, S. K. , Fred
Chen and others did to get the Taiwan
Relations Act into law and create a hard
core of support in the Congress. Even
with all the new Members, the word seems
to have filtered down. I noticed the
spokesperson on the President's trip was
a young man named Jason Yuan.....one of
your students who obviously learned a great
deal from his seniors. His quotes were
excellent so please give him my best regards and compliments when you see him.

I want to come to Taiwan!

Sincerely,

10955 Wurzbach Rd., # 104
San Antonio, Texas 78230

December 20, 1995

Dear C.P.:

Received your holiday card and note. Delighted
I can look forward to a long lunch with you in San
Diego.

Could you let me know which evening you do your
"cooking." Juli will arrive on Friday, 16 February
but must return to San Antonio on Sunday, the 18th
(early afternoon) because of her schedule at work.
Don't change any plan for us but just let me know
which night is your big dinner!

I expect to arrive in San Diego on the afternoon
of Thursday, 15 February and will give you a call
after I get in.

Sincerely

中 歐 貿 易 促 進 會
EURO-ASIA TRADE ORGANIZATION

January 12, 1996

Mr. Dayle Henington
10955 Wurzbach Road, #104
San Antonio, Texas 78230
U. S. A.

Dear Dayle:

I have received your letter of Dec. 20, 1995 and deeply regret to inform you that I am forced to cancel my trip to the U.S. and shall miss the opportunity of our reunion at Michele's home on Chinese New Year Eve.

The main reason is that in the past two years I had suffered a few sudden seizures of serious dizziness because of viewing all the objects turning round and round for a few minutes. My doctor said it was caused by the unbalancing of eardrum, and there was no alarm on my health.

But last week, I had such seizure again except this time all the objects turning clockwise slowly without stopping. So I went to see an ENT specialist and had a thorough examination. The doctor said the illness was caused by inadequate blood circulation originating from my right shoulder and spine. I asked for the reason and received the same discouraging answer: Aging. How disheartening!

The good news is that I am recovering very well, but the bad news is that I should not travel for at least two months. Therefore, I propose to postpone our Chinese New Year Eve Dinner in 1997. I promise I won't be ill again next time.

Wishing you and Juli all the best in 1996.

Sincerely,

C. P.

C. P. Chang

10955 Wurzbach Road, # 104
San Antonio, Texas 78230

August 12, 1996

Dear C.P.,

It was great to have your letter of July 3
and to know you are making a good recovery by
following the advice of your doctor as well as
the tender loving care you always recieve from
Cecilia. We are lucky guys C. P. to have such
wonderful spouses.

I have not heard from Rogers recently but
will be alert to his suggestion of a discussion
meeting in the Atlanta area. I have long known
of the distinguished law firm Lee & Li and I am
sure there will be much interest in many areas
as to how to make the Chines connection. It seems
that Texas is so focused on the NAFTA treaty and
its unfolding opportunities that most of the focus
is on Mexico.

Juli and I have a short trip planned to Italy
in early October so I hope that your visit to the
states will be in later October. In any event,
let me know the dates and locations when you know
them because I do not want to miss an opportunity to
see you.

Since Juli will terminate her employment at the
end of the year, I will want to discuss with you a
good time to visit Taipei after the first of the year.
Juli has never been in that part of the world so I
must get her there soon.

I enjoyed the update of John and Nina and their
family. I will look forward to a re-union of the
old C.P. clan in Taipei in 1997. In the meantime,
Our love to you both and keep in touch. Be sure
you have our phone number in San Antonio which is
Area Code 210/558-8639.

Your friend,

EDINGTON, WADE & ASSOCIATES, INC.
FOURTEEN PIEDMONT CENTER
SUITE 1510
ATLANTA, GEORGIA 30305

WILLIAM H. EDINGTON
T. ROGERS WADE
WILLIAM P. DUBOSE
JAMES L. MORGAN
ELAINE C. NACHMAN

404-262-0888
FAX 404-262-1726

ALEXANDRIA OFFICE
803 PRINCE STREET
ALEXANDRIA, VIRGINIA 22314
703-836-3328
FAX 703-836-1403

May 25, 1996

Hon. C.P. Chang
Euro-Asia Trade Organization
3rd Floor, 9 Roosevelt Road
Section 2
Taipei, Taiwan R.O.C.

Dear C.P.:

Our friend, Dayle Henington, visited with Marcia and I last Fall and, needless
to say, we talked alot about you and our years in Washington. He was
looking forward to your trip to the U.S. for Chinese New Year and I know he
and Julie were greatly disappointed that you were unable to be here. He shared
your letter with me and I hope that all is well with your health. You need to take
good care of yourself so we can all get together again soon.

Marcia and I think of the good friends we had in those days and often wonder
how you and your family are doing . We have been back in Atlanta
since 1979, but I am in Washington several times a month. My business is
still dealing with the government (both State and Federal) and we have offices
in Atlanta and Washington. Do you ever see John and Nina Fang? I suppose
their "little children" are all grown-up, but you remember that I first met them on
my trip to Taiwan before they were married. Time certainly is flying away from
us! I hope we will all get together (either here or there) soon.

Please let me know when you will be coming this way and we will get with Dayle
and Julie to plan a "party".

With best wishes to you and your family, I am,

Your friend,

Rogers Wade

143

Mr. Rogers Wade
Edinton, Wade & Associates, Inc.
Fourteen Piedmont Center
Suite 1510
Atlanta, Georgia 30305
U.S.A.   July 3, 1996

Dear Rogers:

It was such a pleasant surprise to receive your letter of May 25,1996. Time is certainly flying from us and your warm greetings remind me of the good old days when I was working with our embassy in Washington, D.C. where we spent a lot of happy time together in the seventies.

Although I have not communicated with you for a long time, I have heard of your good work in Georgia from Dayle Henington with whom I have kept in touch over the past 20 years. Since Dayle left Washington, D.C., it seems my last connection with that beautiful city has been cut off. How heartening and nostalgic every time I thought of D.C. It was once my battleground where I fought the hardest battle in my life and won the hearts of so many good friends, both conservatives and liberals. There is no doubt that my Washington experience has helped me not only to widen my horizon and vision of world outlook, but also to shape my course in life. On the other hand, I had also learned so much from all of my good friends from the Capitol Hill about American decency as well as American toughness. And you are among the top of the list. Thank you, Rogers !

John Feng and Nina are doing well in Taipei. Nina is now Marketing Manager of IBM Taiwan and making a lot more money than John. However, John is quite active in politics in recent years and seems quite successful in his career with KMT, the ruling party. He is now Managing Director of International Edition, Central Daily News -- KMT's propaganda machine. Concurrently, he is Deputy Director General of Youth Department at the KMT Headquarters. Aside from their success in their respective careers, they are also doing quite well with the family. Can you imagine that their eldest son is going to college in the fall semester, while their younger son .will be in the ninth grade after summer vacation? Their youngest child is a girl and the gem of the family who will be in the fifth grade. So much for John Feng -- the prodigal of our gang.

As to myself, I am now living a semi-retired life in Taipei, but occasionally doing some advisory work as advisor to the Board of Foreign Trade, Ministry of Economic Affairs, as well as advisor to Lee and Li Attorneys-at-Law, the largest law firm in Taipei with a staff of 370 personnel including 150 lawyers.

Since 1992, I have been traveling, by paying my own way, quite often to mainland China, as a devoted Christian doing volunteer work, to give lectures on the subjects of globalization of world economy, impacts of economic and trade integration of the major economic powers in the forms of European Union and NAFTA to the world trade, and the importance of liberalization and internationalization of the economy and trade for the Asian countries, including mainland China. I hope that, through my lectures and seminars, I can help, in a small way, enlighten the mainland Chinese government officials, college teachers and students that Taiwan can share its economic and political reform experience with the mainland. I am more than convinced that Taiwan's experience can be a source of inspiration and aspiration to the mainland Chinese.

Possibly, I will, if my health permits, travel to the U.S. in October with Mr. Dean Chiang, a partner of Lee and Li Attorneys-at-Law, to participate in seminars and discussion meetings for giving our presentations on the topics of "Taiwan as a gateway to American companies to enter the mainland China market", "How to do business and invest in the mainland China," and "The emergence of a greater Chinese Common market and its impacts to the world economy and trade." If you are interested in arranging such a meeting in Atlanta for Georgian businesses and law firms, I'll send our résumés for you to prepare for such an event. And we will be able to get together for a day or two, and perhaps we can ask Dayle to join us for a reunion.

My home address is as follows:
6F, 18-1, Alley 21, Lane 69
Minsheng E. Road, Sec.5
Taipei, Taiwan, R.O.C.
Tel and Fax No. (02) 769-1933

In the meantime, Cecilia and I send you and Marcia our warmest regards.

Sincerely,

C.P. Chang

10955 Wurzbach Rd., # 104
San Antonio, Tx. 78230

October 30, 1996

Dear C.P.:

Rogers Wade called me this week to
see if I had heard anymore about the
possibility of your heading this way
with a member of your law firm. Since
he hadn't heard any more, he was a bit
concerned. Anyway, I hope all is well.

Have had a couple of notes from
Michele about her big cycling challenge
to take place in Tucson on November 23.

Juli and I have had a nice year.
Juli will be retiring from her job in
December and then we will both be free
to travel more together. Since Juli's
daughter is a flight attendant for
United Airlines, we get free flying
privileges and that is great. We want
to plan a trip to Asia in 1997 and will
coordinate with you about the best time
to be able to see my best friend in that
part of the world! Love to you and
Cecilia.

[signature]

10955 Wurzbach Road, # 104
San Antonio, Texas 78230

December 17, 1996

Dear C. P.,

There has been so much in our news of late about
the China relationship, how I wish I could have an
evening with you so I could understand all that is
taking place. I was especially interested in this
man C. H. Tung and the Newsweek article I am enclosing
preceded the formal announcement of his appointment.
It would seem to me that the Clinton Administration is
in over it's head in dealing with the Chinese officials.
I don't feel comfortable that they have a C.P. Chang
on their staff to help them understand the complexities!

Rogers Wade called me recently to find out if I
had heard from you concerning a tentatively planned trip
to the states with your law firm. He did hope that all
was well with you. Since Michelle and I have kept in
touch through correspondence, I told him I thought I
would have heard from here if anything was amiss.

1997 is the year for a visit to your part of the
world. The thinking now is during the summer or fall
but I would want to have a general idea from you as to
the best time for us to spend time with you and Cecilia
because that would be the primary reason for the trip.
Juli has never been to Asia so I would try to show her
Hong Kong and Singapore while in your part of the world.
Not interested in Tokyo. Perhaps Bangkok, although I
understand it is chaos and most people just pass through!

Juli and I are leaving just after Christmas for
a couple of weeks in Italy, visiting a friend in
Sicily. When we return mid-January, I hope I will have
a letter from you bringing me up to date on your recovery
and the tender loving care you get from Cecilia. Love
to you both.

Love —

P.S.
Send photo of you
+ Cecilia.

147

Dear C. P. + Cecilia,

I wanted you to see a photograph of your
dinner guests in San Diego this past July! It's
too bad the host couldn't be with us because as
you can see there is much happiness in the faces
of the guests.How wonderful to have the chance
to not only visit with Michelle but to see
Cecilia as well.

Soon I am going to call United Air Lines
to find out when they will permit Juli and I
to travel to Taiwan next year. Since we will
be using free tickets for our trip, we must
select from the dates available and I asked
Michelle if she would tell us which months are
best, which are fair and if there are some months
one shouldn't come at all! Then, we will have
some guide when we call up United. We want to
make several side trips while we are in your
part of the world...Hong Kong, perhaps Singapore
and Tokyo briefly. Do you think we should try
to arrange a trip to Big China from Hong Kong?

Taiwan was in the news today. I am enclosing
two clippings.

Juli's father came to Chicago from Slovakia
when he was 14. All of his family remained in
the old country. Juli has 36 cousins and 3 aunts
there and we are going to visit them next week.
She is very excited.

C. P. Give Cecilia my love and tell her again
how much we enjoyed our visit with her. She is as
beautiful as ever....how did you ever manage to
capture such a fantastic person? We think of you
as very special friends and count the months until
we see you. Should you plan a San Diego trip to
cook a fish, please let me know so I can come out!

Sincerely, your friend
Doyle

MARSHALL L. LYNAM
6423 Lee Highway
Arlington, Virginia 22205

June 12, 1999

Dear C. P.

Dayle was thoughtful enough to send me a copy of your letter about your successful heart surgery, and I want to tell you how delighted I am that you came through with such flying colors!

It was wonderful to hear from you, even second-hand. I think often about you and the exciting and interesting times that we have had together. One of the wisest things your country ever did was to send C. P. Chang to represent them in Washington!

To borrow a quote from Goldsmith, I love everything that's old — old friends, old times, old manners, old books, old wine... and old friends are the best! So you be sure to take care of yourself, OK? And I'm going to offer a prayer for your continued good health.

Since Jim Wright left Congress, I have been here as a consultant representing Dallas/Fort Worth International Airport and Tandy/Radio Shacks. I also have written a little book, and in case you haven't seen it I am sending you a copy. It's strictly a feel-good, fun book, and I hope you like it. Eddie joins me in wishing all the best to you and Cecilia.

Warm regards

Marshall

149

June 21, 1999

Dear Marshall:

I was extremely delighted to receive your heartwarming letter of June 12, 1999, together with your fine book《Stories I Ever Told the Speaker》. It was most thoughtful of you to write me and send your best wishes. Thank you so much, my dear friend.

On June 7, I was admitted to hospital again for the surgery on the narrowed artery of my right-side neck. However, after a series of tests in five days, for the preparation of my surgery, a panel of doctors, including a visiting American specialist renowned in this field, held a unanimous opinion that my present condition did not call for an immediate surgery. And I was thus discharged from hospital in good shape. Thank God for His mercy and grace in sparing me another surgery. Obviously, your prayer and ours had been heard and answered by the good Lord who has been very kind to watch over me and keep me from falling apart.

Last night, I started to read your book devouring word after word with great admiration for your honest, savvy, but wicked style of writing. It brought me back to many fond memories of 50s, 60s and 70s when I was living in the United States on different missions. And then I was homesick and stayed awake on bed for hours in thinking of you and many old friends. In particular, I thought and reminisced about those wonderful, exciting, but turbulent years of 1974-1978 when I worked, sweated and laughed with you and my pals in the U. S. Congress in Washington, D. C. When returning to Taiwan in 1978, a part of me was left over in that beautiful city forever.

I am grateful that Marshall Lynam has come across my path in the course of serving my country in Washington. Your friendship and support helped make my tour of duty at our Embassy in your nation's capital the highlight of my government service as well as the finest hour of my humble life. You and Dayle Henington were my guiding angels to teach me about American politics and to open many doors in both the House and Senate for me. Indeed, I really learned fast, fast enough to make me feel almost a part of your institution—the Congress, not to mention the way I drank with you and became a "shooter" myself.

Dear Marshall, I want you to know that I have promised to God that I am decidedly going to improve my health with more exercises, a strict diet and a lot of church activities (I am a senior deacon at my Baptist Church) so that I can devote my remaining days on earth to glorifying Him through spreading the Gospel and being a witness to His mercy and grace given to those who have faith in Him.

In closing this letter, I am enclosing a copy of 《My New Year Prayer》 by an unknown author with a prayer for your good health and much happiness. May God be with you and your lovely family.

Cecilia joins me in sending you and Eddie our love and warmest regards.

Sincerely,

C. P.

P. S. A copy of this letter will be sent to Dayle.

2000s

二〇〇〇年五月台灣出現首次的政黨輪替，這不僅標誌台灣在國內政治發展上的重要階段，也是台灣在推動對外關係上的新開始，在推動對外關係的內涵跟策略上，也開始呈現不同的面貌，其中「全民外交」、「民主外交」、「人權外交」等的提出，都反映出新的執政者試圖以新思維與新作法，為台灣找尋國際出路的努力。終於，在二〇〇二年一月一日終於成為世界貿易組織（WTO）的正式會員國。

Dear Dayle:

Welcome to the club! You should be thankful to the early warning of cardiovascular disease, for one-third of the people who suffered a massive heart attack and died did not know they had a heart problem. Your doctor was alert and quick to detect the hidden danger and sent you to the hospital for examination. A lot of people were not so lucky that when the attack came, it was either too late to be treated in a hospital or they had to undergo a by-pass surgery.

Like you, I had my early warning in 1987, thanks to our good Lord. Since then, I have paid much attention to my diet and started to exercise regularly. This helped to slow down the narrowing process of my right artery until the Chinese New Year of 1999 when I started to feel chest pain and became very weak. Immediately my doctor sent me to hospitalization and to undergo an angioplasty operation (ballooning of the narrowed artery). It took only three days and I had fully recovered without having to take the risk of a by-pass surgery. Therefore, in your case, I don't think you would ever need such a surgery. Like me in 1987, your blockages are small enough to require treating with medication and diet only. Still, you need to keep track of the development of your narrowed artery so that, if it gets worse, you could always have a timely angioplasty operation which is much safer.

Looking back to our past lives, we both should feel grateful for having lived a full, rich life, though there had been occasionally ups and downs. Yes, we worked hard and served our country well. Nevertheless, we had also learned the hard lesson of surviving in the jungle of politics and made a wise decision to quit while we were still in the prime of our lives to start a new career in the field of trade promotion in which we had also excelled.

I am grateful that Dayle Henington had crossed my paths when I was working in Washington, D. C. in the 70s for my last assignment in the government service. It seemed that we hit it together in the very beginning of our friendship which has lasted well over a quarter of century. Now we are both aging and finding ourselves no longer enthusiastic in politics as we did years ago. We should be so, for we had had our day in fighting for our common cause and, at the same time, enjoyed our frequent get-togethers in the exciting Washington politics. Indeed, we can look back with pride and satisfaction to say: "This was the finest hour in my life."

Nevertheless, I am still worrying about the present political chaos in Taiwan. It was so ironic that Taiwan people should have, while getting rid of the corrupt and senile KMT, voted an extremist DPP (the opposition party) candidate to become our new president with a minority seat in the Legislative Yuan. For the first time in Taiwan, we now have a new administration full of inexperienced, arrogant Red Guards or leftists who devote themselves to overturning everything we have cherished for. In the process, Taiwan's economy has been spinning spirally downward, resulting in the exodus of industries to mainland China and Southeast Asia. Consequently, we are now facing an unprecedented unemployment crisis with an all-time high of 3.3%, while the index of the stock market has plunged 50% since the inception of the new government on May 20, 2000.

What does all this mean? Recently, I have begun to think that probably the leader of a country embodies the collective unconsciousness of his people. Can it be that after the long reins of KMT's authoritarian rule for over 50 years, people had been yearning for a change and were willing to take a risk by choosing the opposition leader to run the country, even though the opposition was noted for its dogmatic, radical belief in anti-growth economic policy and passion for Taiwan independence.

Anyway, we were doing well at removing a lousy government, and I am confident that we will also be able to remove the present lousy government in 2004. We are a young republic and we are maturing as a democracy. Getting KMT out of office has not solved our problems, but it could be the beginning of a real change. For Taiwan people have learned a lesson and will be more cautious and wise in choosing their leader next time around. In fact, our new president had already accepted the hard reality and taken a series of conciliatory steps to make and mend with the Legislative Yuan and the public opinion.

So much for Taiwan politics! I hope that I have given you a glimpse of Taiwan's political development which is a far cry from that of the 70s and the 80s you used to know. In the meantime, Cecilia joins me in sending you and Juli our warmest regards.

C. P.

10955 Wurzbach Rd # 104
San Antonio, Tx 78230

May 27, 2003

Dear C. P.,

    If you received a letter from me
everytime I think of you, your mail box
would be full all the time. With
everyone mostly doing e-mail, old
fashioned letters like the ones you and I
have exchanged over the years are becoming
rare indeed. But yesterday, we had an
e-mail from Michelle saying hello and
advising us that Cecelia was visiting her
through August and that perhaps you might
get lonesome enough for them to show up
in San Diego yourself!

    I don't want you to be lonesome but
I do hope you might decide to make the
trip because if you do, I would certainly
fly out to San Diego for the chance to
see you again. Juli and I have continued
to travel quite a bit since we have
flight privileges on United because of
Juli's daughter being a flight attendant.
With all of their problems, we thought
the privileges might end but so far not.
Michelle mentioned the death in your
family and I send my condolence. I
have only nephews left on my side and I
have lost several older friends in recent
years. As we move to the front of the
line, it seems impossible that so many years
have past.

    While the world has alwayas been a
treacherous place, it seems now that our
quality of life is way down. I'm sorry
for the young people like Michelle and

I get to Washington from time to time. Recently, some friends hosted an event for Juli and me.....our 20th Anniversary and it was a nice time. While driving up Mass Avenue, I passed your old office and remembered our many visits there with John and S. K. Hu. I also remember picking up the cheap booze that allowed me to entertain like I was a diplomat myslef!

Someone told me that John Feng has been given an Ambassadorial appointment. Is that true and if so, where is he in case I should go there.

I wanted to say hello to you my friend. I do hope you decide to come this way. Take care of yourself. Juli joins me in sending much love to you.

Dear Dayle:

It is always a pleasant surprise to receive your letter which brings me back to another time and another place. True, we had had some of the best years few could ever expect, and we had lived a full, rich life of such diverse and rewarding careers. Indeed, we should be thankful to our good Lord for His blessing in giving us a pleasant retired life.

I was very happy to hear that you and Juli had just celebrated your 20th anniversary. Otherwise, I would never have my peace of mind, whenever, in thinking of my old pale Dayle living a lonely life alone at old age. I sincerely believe that Juli is a godsend angel, for God remembers your great contributions in dedicating yourself to the public service as well as to your loyalty to colleagues and friends

2002 was a bad year for me, for I had lost several aged relatives and old friends in both Taiwan and mainland China, including several buddies in the class of 1952 of the Naval Academy. It was the first time that I had been hit so hard by the death of so many loved ones. Consequently, I went into depression for a while, but I had managed to ride out of the deep grief. So when I learned the news of my brother's sudden death in May, I was full of gratitude to God for His mercy in letting my brother die in such a peaceful manner that it was only a few seconds after getting up from his nap and then he passed away without any pain. He was 80 and had lived a good life as compared to others in Communist China. The only regret was that I was prevented from going to Shanghai to attend his funeral because of SARS. For Shanghai requires quarantine of 14 days for visitors from Taiwan, while Taiwan imposes quarantine of 10 days for anyone coming from mainland China, What an irony!

John has been given an ambassadorial appointment to Dominica and he will arrive at his new post in July. I plan to invite him for lunch to say farewell and I'll tell him to be prepared for a surprise visit from you and Juli in Dominica which seems not too far away from Texas.

Dear Dayle, since I am reaching 75, I tend to be reluctant to take a long flight of 11-13 hours to San Diego. I'd rather have Michele to visit us in Taipei or to travel to mainland China together. But I'll definitely visit the U. S. in 2005 to attend my granddaughter's graduation from high school. Then we will be able to get together again, and I'll most certainly fulfill my promise of cooking you and Juli a hot chilly fish dinner.

Please send my love to Juli. You'll always be in my prayers.

C. P.

10955 Wurzbach Road, # 104
San Antonio, Texas 78230

July 15, 2003

Dear C.P.,

    I do not want to burden you with my correspondence
and it will be okay if you place this letter in your diary
for a response in the fall! I just wanted to tell you
that I shared your wonderful letter of June 12th with
Rogers Wade and Marshall Lynam and their responses are
enclosed for I knew you would enjoy reading their admiring
words.

    Since moving back to Texas in late '94, I have had
fairly frequent visits with Marshall when I would go to
Washington or he would come to Texas. As for Rogers, I've
really only had one good visit with him in the past
several years but we manage to keep in touch with letters
and e-mails. As you could read, Marshall will be returning
to Texas in the fall and I am glad he will be closer so we
can, hopefully, visit more often. Marshall is ahead of us,
C. P., in years. He is close to 80 now.

    Hopefully, you have had your farewell lunch with John
and he is now in Dominica. We certainly hope it will be
possible for us to get there for a visit. I will have to
remind him that all the wise things he knows, he learned
from one of us! Ha.

    I was sorry to learn of your loss of dear family.
My parents, brother and sister, have been gone many years
now but they are in my thoughts constantly. The joy of all
good memories are nice to have when I think of them. But
I did want to share with you two items that have always been
favorites of mine. First, the minister's article on
"seniority" which both you and I have and then the second,
a poem by William Randolph Hearst...."The Song of the River."
I know you will enjoy them both.

    My friend, I think of you all the time and know that
we will have a big re-union in 2005, if not sooner. Juli
joins me in sending much love.

Dayle

159

1215 N. Waterman, # 1-K
Arlington Heights, Il 60004

August 2, 2006

Dear C.P.,

I am looking at the photos taken during our last visit
in San Diego. We all look so happy and we were. I
certainly treasured that opportunity to have some time
with you and Cecilia . Both of us have arrived at the
point in life where time has a much different significance
than in our younger years. Surely we are destined to
make it well into our 80's so that we will get to plan
another visit together.

Juli and I have enjoyed being in Chicago. Our ten years
in Texas were also enjoyable but Chicago has so many more
cultural options and our travel on United is easier from
here. Do you remember that since Juli's (our) daughter
works for United Airlines, we are extended flight privileges
at little or no expense. We just completed a 5 day trip
to Alaska where I was assigned with the Air Force from 1955-
58 so it was my first return in 48 years! Elmendorf AFB
looked a bit different than the pictures in my mind and it
was enjoyable to see again the spectacular scenery.

I am wondering what you are doing with your time these days.
Are you will hiking with your friends and just living the
quiet, contented life? In the spring, I decided I needed
to pay attention to my weight and in the intervening months,
I have lost 40 pounds and continuing to go down to a desired
weight of 205 or so. I'm proud of the effort but, of course,
couldn't have done it without Juli's loving hands directing
my diet. I haven't talked to Michelle recently so hope all
is well there. Have not been back to San Diego since our
visit. Do you remember or perhaps I didn't tell you that
last April during a holiday in Hawaii I had an electrical
malfunction in my heart and received the implant of a pace-
maker. It has worked wonderfully and I am feeling great.

I am sick to death of my country's leadership and particularly
the dieing of so many young men in Iraq. Just as we were
getting ready to fly hom from Alaska, it was announced that
a large Alaskan Army contingent would be extended for many
months as they prepared to come home. They are being moved
into Baghdad where there will surely be many deaths.

If you have the time and energy, I would love to hear from
you and will share the letter with Marshall and Rogers as
they always ask me if I have heard from you. Love to you
and Cecilia from Juli and me. Your friend,

Oct. 12, 2006

Dear Dayle:

Please forgive me for not writing you sooner to reply your heart-warming letter of August 2, 2006. Only because I wanted to write you a nice and long letter in a right mood and fine spirit. It seems it never happened and so I made excuses for stalling. Finally, the moment arrived on the night of October 6—the Chinese Mid-Autumn Festival, when I was watching and enjoying Celine Dion's concert DVD. When she came to sing "The First Time I Saw Your Face," I was struck with deep emotion and sank into an old man's reminiscence. I vividly remembered it was the first time I had heard this beautiful song at a colonial-style restaurant of the resort lodge on the top of the Blue Ridge Mountain, overlooking the twinkling-stars-filled Shennandoah Valley. The lady singer wore a 19th-century Virginian costume and sang beautifully. It was our first vacation in America and it was a fine day in October in 1976. Michele was only sixteen and I was only, my God, 47 then. Sometimes I really couldn't believe I was approaching 80. So this song brought me back to another time and another place. And, naturally, I started to think of my Washington years in the seventies and I felt so nostalgic and thought a lot of Dale Henington, Marshall Lynam, Rogers Wade, Shirley Boehlert and a lot of other pals. But before I start this long letter, I need to fix a drink of Majito to warm me up, for it's after five now; and I observe this rule strictly. Pause!!

Ha, Ha, it's much better to continue writing to you while sipping the Mojito. I remember dearly that you taught me to drink Gin Tonic with the emphasis on taking Vodka (instead of Gin) in summer. But last year in San Diego when we had dinner together with Cecilia and Michele, you only ordered one Gin Tonic, but I had two Martinis (straight) to celebrate our reunion. Dayle, I am so grateful whenever I think that you had flown all the way from Chicago to see me and to cheer me up during my short and sad stay in California attending my brother-in-law's funeral. He was also my classmate in the class of 1952, Naval Academy. It's sad to mention that I have lost almost one-third of my 186 buddies and that I was often asked

161

to give a eulogy at the funeral. I hated to do this, but they said my eulogy was eloquent and moving. How ironic! It was only not too many years ago that I was often asked to give a congratulatory message at the wedding banquet of my buddies' children. On one occasion, I even had to give two speeches in Chinese and English, because the bridegroom's parents are Malaysian Chinese who do not speak Mandarin.

So sorry, Dayle, I have a bit too indulged myself in my sorrowful sentiments. I am writing this letter off and on, and its ten-thirty in the night and I need to fix a scotch on-the-rock to give me more inspiration to talk to you. To tell you frankly, I have become so lazy that I rarely write anything in recent years. This is only my fourth letter in 2006, but I am in the mood to write you and I feel very happy.

Happy as I am, now I am going to talk about my deep-in-my-heart feeling about my memory of and gratitude to Washington, D.C. and to my congressional friends. You know very well that I am not the bragging type; however, tonight, I very much want to brag about my hard-earned experience and achievement in the four memorable years of my diplomatic service in Washington, D.C. Looking back I clearly see these years as the best years of my life and the finest hour of my government career. For it was the Capitol Hill and my congressional friends that had helped groom me and educate me to do a bigger job—promoting Taiwan's economic and trade relations wit European countries. I'll elaborate upon this subject later.

Undoubtedly, working on the Capitol Hill was, in every respect, a sort of boot-camp training and my congressional friends were like drill sergeants. Never had in my life I learned so much and made so many friends in such a short period (about one hundred). They were well educated and highly motivated, and they were always in a hurry. Some of them were cynical and arrogant, but most of them were friendly and decent. It was only after a number of years that I had realized that I had learned and inherited from my congressional friends the American toughness and American decency.

Equipped with this American toughness and American decency, I thus feared no one in any dialogue with European trade officials, parliamentarians, business leaders and bankers throughout my sixteen years of countless travels to European capitals and major cities, including Eastern Europe in 90's. but, most important of all, I had, through my close association and friendship with congressional aides, learned the art and the essence of a meaningful debate—never try to argue with the other's mind, but try to reach his heart.

As I moved into my sixties, I had become wiser, wittier and more mellowed. On occasions, I could even be naughty. One year in Paris, Credit Lyonnais hosted a dinner in honor of me. After a few glasses of fine French wine, I started to crack a joke about the president of the largest bank in a small town of mid-America. At the end of the story, (I'll give you the details over the phone) my French hosts laughed their heads off. Then, I said slowly that I was going to Zurich tomorrow and I would tell the same joke to my Swiss friends except that the American bank will be changed into a French bank. Instantly, everyone gasped and shouted "No." In saying farewell, a chic woman executive kissed my cheek and whispered, "Please tell the Swiss, it's a German bank."

To the British, I was a jolly good old chap. It was easy for me to handle the snobbish and cynical ones. All I had to do was to mention that I had been a trainee in the Royal Navy for 18 months in 1947 – 1948. It always worked, for, instantly, they were awed and pleased with my credential. They surely loved and revered their once-glorious Royal Navy.

What a career! What a life! In gratitude, I let Cecilia take me to te church and was converted to Christianity. Presently, I am the chairman of my church's board of directors and the chairman of the man's department, as well as the moderator of the weekly reading meeting. I'll continue to serve the Good Lord for the rest of my life.

So long, my dear friend. I'll write you again about China in 2007.

Cecilia joins me in wishing you and Julie all the best.

163

C.P.

P.S. Copy to Michele

November 1, 2006

On Tuesday, October 24, Juli answered a call at about 9:15 a.m., and I heard her exclaim, "C.P., how great to hear your voice!" She shortly passed me the phone and C.P. anxiously said, "Did you receive my letter?" I told him no, I had not and he excitedly told me that he had mailed me a letter by "fast" mail and had mailed a copy of the letter to his daughter, Michelle, in San Diego who had been our intermediary for years. Michelle had received the letter the day before and he asked what was wrong with our postal service! I told him it would probably take an additional day to come from California to Illinois and he said he was calling to tell me the joke that he could not report in his letter. He said he would call me again on Thursday morning, when hopefully, with his letter in my hand, he could tell me the joke. Well, that certainly peaked my interest and, wouldn't you know, two hours later his letter arrived in our morning mail.

After reading his letter, I became more anxious to hear this joke. Then, on Thursday morning, again about 9:15 a.m. (10:15 p.m. in Taipei), the phone rang and it was C.P. From that time to about 9:30 a.m. (it was at least 15 minutes) he told me his joke. Unfortunately, it is a story that must be told slowly, with great embellishment, so you must wait until again we meet to hear this story. Don't forget to have me tell it. I have made notes to help remember the details!

C.P. had told me before that he just didn't write many letters anymore and even with their daughter in San Diego, they mostly communicated by telephone or visits to each other's homes. But in recent years, C.P. said he didn't enjoy the long flights anymore and so, it usually was Cecelia who made the trips to San Diego. In 2005 I hopped over to San Diego during his last visit there and we had a great reunion. I know we would all agree that he is one of the most unique persons any of us have ever met and as good a friend as any of us have ever had. He asked me to be sure you all (Rogers Wade, Marshall Lynam and Sherry Boehlert) received copies of the letter which was meant for all of us. I gave him an update on each of you and he, again, stressed what wonderful friends you all were to him.

During all of this, of course, I thought of these friendships we have shared and what treasures they are in my memory. Most of my friendships, close friendships, originated so many years ago and become more special when one realizes they were made at a special time in life.

I hope all of you are well and that we will meet again soon. Love to Eddie Lynam, Marcia Wade and Mary Ann Boehlert.

Dayle

P.S. Enjoy C.P.'s letter and consider sending him a not to tell him, "Henington delivered."

C. P. Chang (Cecelia)
Ming Shen East Road
Section 5, Lane 21, 18-1 6F
Taipei, Taiwan
Republic of China

Dear C.P. —

Since your Christmas note brought us joy, I have no
excuse for not answering sooner. The photo of you, Cecilia
and Michelle reminds me of my good fortune to cross paths
with your family during our Washington tours. The
many lunches and times in your lovely home are all in place
in my mind and I thhink of you all the time!

As you know, we are in an election cycle and I'm wondering
if Taiwan has a favorite. It seems to me that Bush was
a little wishy-washy about U. S. policy toward Taiwan
but maybe you had a different impression there. In any
case, I am pleased we will be making a change next January
because our country has a lot of repairing to do with our
friends and foes. The article I've enclosed on your
recent election seems to indicate perhaps a change there is
in progress.

We try and keep in touch with Michelle and earlier this
year, we were so disappointed that we had a trip planned
when she advised us she would be in Chicago for a meeting.
So, sometime in the spring we will go to San Diego and look
forward to a visit with her. I know you and Cecilia must
miss her terribly. Now that we are back in Chicago, Juli
gets frequent visits with daughter Chris, who still flies
for United Airlines, which gets us flight privileges
for very low cost.

I often think of Fred Chin and John and wonder if you are
still in touch with them. There is some sad news concerning
Marshall Lynam. He has been diagnosed with early Alzimers
and while they had moved back to Ft. Worth Texas a couple
of years ago, Marshall's wife Eddie decided to return them
to Virginia because she feels they would be better off.

I continue to enjoy good health. Early in the year I lost
58 pounds and have been going to the health club and
maintaining my weight at around 200! We have actually had
fewer colds and coughs in Chicago than we had in Texas.
My friend, I pray there will be another chance for us to
meet one of these days. In the meantime, know that you
and Cecilia are in our regular thoughts and we treasure
your friendship.

All the best,

Dayle

166

1215 N. Waterman Ave., # 1-K
Arlington Heights, IL 60009

December 8, 2009

Dear C. P.:

For some time I have meant to compose a letter
to Fred Chien and have finally done so. I am enclosing
it with the request that you forward it to him for me.
I believe I sent you a copy of Admiral Lyons article in
the Washington Times. If not, you can read the one I have
enclosed before you mail it to Fred.

Rarely does a day go by when my happiest thoughts
are ꜟNOT those that come from my my reflection on the special
frienships that have shaped my life and thinking. We are
so fortunate to have been able to keep in touch through
the years and I believe that we would like nothing better
than to be able to get together on Saturday mornings and
come up with answers to all the world's problems!
Your wonderful daughter has filled me in on you and Cecilia
from time to time and then I treasure seeing an air mail
letter from Taipei from C. P. Chang!

I will appreciate your sending the enclosed letter
and enclosure along to Ambassador Chien.

Juli and I sned much love for you and Cecilia for
this holiday season.

With love and affection

P. S. The book review from the New York Times on
Madame Chian is for your. The Photo I enclosed of
me with Ambassador Chien is enclosed to go to him
with my letter so that he can recall me after all
the years.

C. P. Chang
6th Floor, # 18-1, Alley 21, Lane 69
Section 5, Min-sheng East Road, Taipei 105
Taiwan, ROC

February 21, 2010

Dear Dayle:

Upon receiving your heartwarming letter of January 19, 2010, I fell into the reminiscence of another era which seemed so far away and, yet, so very close to my heart because I was presently writing, off and on, about the 1970s for my memoirs to be published later this year.

A few days ago, I started to write about the year of 1977 when I was serving as First Secretary of the ROC Embassy in Washington, D. C. Jimmy Carter was then the newly elected president of the United States. Confessing that he was a born-again Christian, he was proud and arrogant. Carter had a biased view toward the ROC government, and so were his liberal Democratic friends in the House of Representatives.

All of a sudden, Congressman Hamilton, Chairman of the House International Affairs Committee, was going to hold a "Taiwan Human Right Hearing." Since Mayor Y. Y. Wang of Kaohsiung City with a population of over a million people was visiting Plains, Georgia, with a population of over a few thousand people, to sign a sister city accord, he was asked to represent the ROC government to testify at the hearing.

I was assigned to escort him to the hearing, and I vividly remembered that I consulted with you and sought your assistance. Your instructions were:
1. Enter the House of Representatives through the X driveway of X parking entrance.
2. Park may car at the X parking space which was your assigned parking lot.
3. Take the nearby elevator to your office where you'll wait for us, even though it was a Saturday afternoon.
4. You will escort us to the House floor.

When I drove Mayor Wang and his assistant to the House, we saw a big crowd of hundreds of anti-ROC government Taiwanese students gathering at the door of House entrance, waiving flags and shouting. The city police force was also shouting to the crowd in order to maintain order.

Upon entering the floor and walking to the stage through the center aisle, I saw, on the left side, a crowd of angry pro-independence students who cursed Mayor Wang:

"Taiwan Traitor!" On the right side, I saw a crowd of pro-ROC government students who greeted and patted a frightened Mayor Wang with encouraging words. House police officers were trying to maintain the order and threatening to throw some of the over-jealous guys out. While I was walking Mayor Wang to the steps of the stage, my heart was broken in seeing the deep schism between the two groups of young Chinese students from Taiwan. It was a very sad moment of my life.

During the hearing, two Taiwanese students testified and accused the ROC government of dictatorship. A Taiwanese lady from the Library of Congress translated accurately. However, when Mayor Wang took the witness stand and testified, she twisted his words. Suddenly, someone in the audience shouted: "Protest!" Chairman Hamilton was displeased and asked the shouting guy to stand up and identify himself. A short and stout young man stood up and declared himself as Professor Huang in University of North Carolina. Hamilton then politely asked him whether he was willing to translate, and the answer was affirmative. So Professor Huang took over and translated Mayor Wang's testimony all the way without any protest.

Also in 1977, with the assistance and introduction of a congressional friend, I went to Atlanta, Georgia, to meet two old associates of Jimmy Carter when he was Governor of the State of Georgia. I had a long talk with the two southern gentlemen respectively, explaining the position of the Republic of China government in defying the communist threat in the western Pacific and in maintaining freedom of the then 16 million people on Taiwan. They were moved and promised to help our cause by persuading Carter not to give up Taiwan.

In fact, all sectors of the Taiwan society, which had any connections with the American societies in the 50 states and in Washington, D. C., were mobilized to lobby for the cause of defending Taiwan as a political entity. Carter later wrote in his memoirs saying bitterly that he felt the heavy pressure upon him by his old friends and associates in Georgia because of Taiwan's lobbying effort. But, most important of all, U. S. Congress did not approve of giving up Taiwan for the recognition of mainland China. Thus the Taiwan Relations Act was signed by Jimmy Carter and announced on April 10, 1979.

In looking back, I was quite satisfied that I was then a conservative doing a pioneering work in the U. S. Congress. But, on the other hand, I was also a pioneer with a conservative mind. Dear friend, please tell me who I was. Soon, in the next letter, I'll write more about the painful years of 1978-1979 I went through in the process of U. S. de-recognition of the ROC as the legitimate government of China. Our law governs that the government secrecy is valid for 25 years, so I am now free to write about my odyssey as a private citizen to help Vice Minister H. K. Yang's mission in Washington, D. C. You were also a great help to him.

Finally, I enclose a few photos of my younger days in the navy.

Cecilia joins me in sending you and Juli our love. God bless you and your family.

Sincerely,

C. P. Chang

P. S.

Your pictures with your brother and the sheriff brought me back to the John Wayne days in the old Wild West.

血歷史08　PC0179

新銳文創
INDEPEDENT & UNIQUE

飛越太平洋的友情
——與美國國會議員的書信集

作　　者	仉家彪
責任編輯	林泰宏
圖文排版	蔡瑋中、陳宛鈴
封面設計	王嵩賀

出版策劃	新銳文創
發 行 人	宋政坤
法律顧問	毛國樑　律師
製作發行	秀威資訊科技股份有限公司
	114 台北市內湖區瑞光路76巷65號1樓
	電話：+886-2-2796-3638　傳真：+886-2-2796-1377
	服務信箱：service@showwe.com.tw
	http://www.showwe.com.tw
郵政劃撥	19563868　戶名：秀威資訊科技股份有限公司
展售門市	國家書店【松江門市】
	104 台北市中山區松江路209號1樓
	電話：+886-2-2518-0207　傳真：+886-2-2518-0778
網路訂購	秀威網路書店：http://www.bodbooks.com.tw
	國家網路書店：http://www.govbooks.com.tw

I S B N	978-986-6094-33-0
出版日期	2011年10月　初版
定　　價	250元

版權所有・翻印必究（本書如有缺頁、破損或裝訂錯誤，請寄回更換）
Copyright © 2011 by Showwe Information Co., Ltd.
All Rights Reserved

Printed in Taiwan

讀者回函卡

感謝您購買本書，為提升服務品質，請填妥以下資料，將讀者回函卡直接寄回或傳真本公司，收到您的寶貴意見後，我們會收藏記錄及檢討，謝謝！
如您需要了解本公司最新出版書目、購書優惠或企劃活動，歡迎您上網查詢或下載相關資料：http:// www.showwe.com.tw

您購買的書名：_____

出生日期：_____ 年_____ 月_____ 日

學歷：□高中 (含) 以下　　□大專　　□研究所 (含) 以上

職業：□製造業　□金融業　□資訊業　□軍警　□傳播業　□自由業
　　　□服務業　□公務員　□教職　　□學生　□家管　　□其它_____

購書地點：□網路書店　□實體書店　□書展　□郵購　□贈閱　□其他

您從何得知本書的消息？

　□網路書店　□實體書店　□網路搜尋　□電子報　□書訊　□雜誌

　□傳播媒體　□親友推薦　□網站推薦　□部落格　□其他_____

您對本書的評價：(請填代號　1.非常滿意　2.滿意　3.尚可　4.再改進)

　封面設計____　版面編排____　內容____　文／譯筆____　價格____

讀完書後您覺得：

　□很有收穫　□有收穫　□收穫不多　□沒收穫

對我們的建議：_____

_____

_____

_____

請貼
郵票

11466
台北市內湖區瑞光路 76 巷 65 號 1 樓

秀威資訊科技股份有限公司　　　收

BOD 數位出版事業部

....

（請沿線對折寄回，謝謝！）

姓　　名：＿＿＿＿＿＿＿＿＿＿　年齡：＿＿＿＿＿　性別：□女　□男

郵遞區號：□□□□□

地　　址：＿＿＿＿＿＿＿＿＿＿＿＿＿＿＿＿＿＿＿＿＿＿＿＿＿

聯絡電話：(日) ＿＿＿＿＿＿＿＿＿＿＿ (夜) ＿＿＿＿＿＿＿＿＿＿＿

E-mail：＿＿＿＿＿＿＿＿＿＿＿＿＿＿＿＿＿＿＿＿＿＿＿＿＿